Weight]
&
Energy Now

How to take
immediate control
of your physical
health and
well being!

NICHOLAS
DELGADO

Author of Fatigue to Vitality
and Zero Cholesterol Weightloss Cookbook

WEIGHT LOSS
&
ENERGY NOW

Copyright pending 1991

Published in the United States of America
by Delgado Medical
16787 Beach Bl., # 202
Huntington Beach Ca. 92647

ISBN 1-879084-01-5

INTRODUCTION

It is important to you to begin living a healthier, longer and more energetic life, isn't it? This plan is designed for the busy person who believes he or she doesn't have time to do anything about creating a healthier lifestyle. To reach your goal of better health, and a more satisfying life, you need a plan, don't you? This book is an exclusive and effective method for reducing cholesterol and weight FAST!

Here, in my latest book, I'll teach you how to shrink fat cells and explain why most diets fail to lower cholesterol. You'll learn how to lose weight without going hungry. I give you invaluable tips on restaurant dining for energy and health and take you on a simulated supermarket field trip. You'll be amazed at how many delicious foods you can enjoy with confidence.

My step-by-step approach will enable you to lose weight, lower cholesterol, correct "fat" blood and begin a healthier, more satisfying lifestyle. You would like to do better at work, think clearer, feel better, look better and have more energy than ever before, wouldn't you? No matter how old you are, or what kind of shape you're in, this book will have something for you.

Find out about the Delgado Cool Tote, our newest aid to help busy people in beginning the program immediately. This lightweight insulated tote comes with a blue ice pack. It stays frozen all day, and enables a busy person like you to carry delicious food with you wherever you go. With the remarkable ideas of this book and the Delgado Cool Tote you'll never be hungry, as you enjoy the healthy food you want, when you want it!

You may not realize it, but you have the power to change your life. You can look forward to a long, healthy life. You don't have to die prematurely from the same diseases that kill over a third of all Americans. There is no mystery here. There is a precise, simple formula to lowering cholesterol and fat in your body. Now we know what's behind the major cause of premature death, and we know there is something we can do about high cholesterol, unwanted weight and even fatigue. Doesn't it make sense to take the first step today toward a healthier and longer life? Good health is a choice. It's a decision you make for yourself, for your family and for your future happiness.

Now you can take part in the complete plan that has been proven effective in preventing and even reversing heart disease, high blood pressure, diabetes, chronic fatigue and obesity. It's worked for me, and for thousands of people like you who have taken control of their lives. Believe me, it also can work for you. Nothing gives me greater joy than to help someone turn their life around and begin living a life that is healthy and more vibrant.

In 1977, as an honors' graduate of the University of Southern California, I began working in critical care units and convalescent hospitals in the field of physical therapy. In those early years, I was discouraged by the lack of progress of those unfortunate patients who were suffering from the ravages of debilitating diseases. I saw patients become progressively worse using conventional methods (excluding low-fat dietary therapy). This led me to a major turning point in my career. I realized that the primary therapy must begin with diet and exercise instead of drugs or surgery. I then studied countless hours reviewing the medical literature in search of the ideal plan. I also understood the need to motivate people to change their diet, so I completed my degree in psychology.

In addition, I began graduate studies in Health Science and Nutrition at Loma Linda University. During this time I was working with Nathan Pritikin as Director of the world renowned Pritikin Better Health Program. Because of my position, I worked with eminent scientists and physicians who were at the forefront of this exciting health education field.

In 1985 I became founder and President of Delgado Medical in Southern California. I helped thousands of patients to lower cholesterol, increase energy, reduce weight and the risk of degenerative diseases. I began hosting my weekly radio show that helped to reach hundreds of thousands of people with the vital information in this book. For the last twelve years I've conducted over 3200 seminars on the topics discussed in this book. I've learned firsthand about the myths that are so prevalent in our society concerning weight and cholesterol content.

This book is dedicated to teaching you up-to-date information that will fit into your busy schedule. You may work more than forty hours a week. You may have children to care for. Most likely you are constantly being tempted with fattening foods, but we have discovered an incredibly easy way for you to enjoy better health. Within two weeks you will notice considerable improvement and within six months no one, not even yourself, can prevent you from succeeding in reaching your goals.

I discovered the key to motivating people. The key is a plan that is easy to understand and follow. The Delgado Plan is the best nutritional program - it takes less time regarding food preparation and allows the flexibility of eating out at fast food establishments and restaurants.

To reach your goals toward better health sucessfully, I suggest you take action by starting this plan today. The rewards you gain will cause you and the people around you to be excited about staying on this program for a lifetime of better health.

FOREWARD

Good health is our birthright. We should live our years actively, in lean, light bodies, with abundant energy, flexibility and muscular strength throughout our span. Along with sensible exercise and emotional happiness, proper diet is essential in creating a state of vibrant health. Fortunately, much progress has been made towards knowing what constitutes ideal nutritional choices - a most excellent presentation of that knowledge is in your hands, right now. In "Weight Loss & Energy Now", Nick Delgado has assembled the best medical and nutritional opinion, plus the fruits of his own vast experience in nutritional counseling, to create a superb, common-sense guide to optimal nutrition through healthful (and delicious!) food choices.

The guidelines presented in this book are based upon sound nutritional science and clinical experience, and reflect the growing awareness that an evolution past our current, high fat, low fiber, animal-based diet is essential if we are to create optimum health. Numerous medical studies now show that common maladies that plague our society - heart disease, high blood pressure, obesity, adult-onset diabetes, gout and other forms of inflammatory joint disease, and other degenerative conditions - are commonly prevented and often improved or actually cured by eating in the dietary style described in the pages to follow.

The human body has absolutely no requirement for the flesh of animals, nor for the milk of cows - and actually functions superbly without these cholesterol-laden, artery-clogging substances. All the protein, vitamins and other nutrients required for human health are abundantly found in the delicious grains, legumes, fruits, vegetables, seeds and other bountiful plants given to us by the Earth - the foundation of the Delgado Health Plan.

In "Weight Loss & Energy Now", Nick Delgado presents sound and practical advice for implementing healthful eating into a busy daily life. Far from a "diet of deprivation," the wonderful ethnic and other cuisines from which these foods are prepared provide a constant parade of taste delights, that are easy to make and satisfying to enjoy. "Weight Loss & Energy Now" and the life-affirming dining style it presents, is a gateway to glowing health, and great eating. I recommend it most highly.

Michael Klaper, M.D.

This book represents the "state-of-the-art" in dietary management of health preservation and disease avoidance (and reversal). Mr. Delgado has taken the principles of diet and exercise fostered by his predecessors and adapted them into a daily living program that is easy, practical and toothsome! This program was formulated with the busy person in mind. Unlike many other books on nutrition, recommendations for food additives, and other artificial remedies, is kept to a minimum. In addition, no guarantees are made for this program — other than optimal nutritional health.

I heartily recommend this book to anyone who is truly serious about preserving health and longevity!

Joseph T. Broderick, MD
Diplomate, American Board
of Internal Medicine

1

FEED YOUR HUNGER THE EASY SOLUTION

Do you want to eat delicious foods (Italian, Mexican, Chinese and American), enjoy frequent meals without hunger, increase your energy and look fit for a lifetime? To have constant energy and achieve your ideal weight, eat lowfat foods just before you get hungry.

Anticipation of hunger is one of the keys to the success of the Delgado Program. It is very important you learn to eat more frequently. We tell our patients to eat just before they get hungry. Be sensitive to that earlier signal of weakness your body sends you about thirty minutes before hunger. It could be a feeling of slight weakness, distraction or an empty feeling in the stomach. On other diets, you're told to fight the natural urge of hunger. Then, finally you're so hungry you lose control and give in to the greasy temptations of our fast-paced environment.

Haven't you ever gone to the supermarket on an empty stomach and noticed how many fattening foods you bought? You know you should eat before going to the market. However, most dieters make a terrible mistake going to a restaurant or relatives house to eat when they're starved. Why not eat (fruits, vegetables or soups) before you go to a restaurant, a friends' or relatives' house for a meal? In this way you will be in control to avoid temptations and make better food choices.

Why do you think fast food restaurants are so successful? Have you noticed how liquor stores and markets have two thirds of the cash register area filled with candy and snacks? At Delgado Medical we have discovered your only protection from this powerful temptation, to control temptation, simply anticipate your hunger. You must eat low calorie, high fiber foods the moment you feel a slight drop in energy or have an empty feeling in the stomach. When you're trying to lose weight, you have to eat a lot more fruits (three to eight pieces a day) and a lot more vegetables - up to 4 lbs. worth (raw, cooked, steamed, microwaved or in soups). Vegetables and fruits are high in water content, so you won't have to drink eight glasses of water a day. Two to four glasses would be sufficient depending on how much you exercise. Many overweight people fear overeating. On the Delgado Plan, a compulsive eater can "overeat" fruits, vegetables, soups and salads and still lose weight. For example, if you consumed 4 lbs. of vegetables and fruit in a day, you would have taken in an average of only 550 calories. There would have been no room left for the fattening foods like meat, cheese, milk, eggs and oils.

An experiment was conducted requiring the participants to eat ten potatoes a day. They could eat anything else, as long as they ate the ten potatoes first (potatoes have only 69 calories each x 10 = 690 calories). The participants all lost fat weight during the three month experiment. There was little room for any other food! Of course, the Delgado Plan encourages you to eat a variety of natural foods, not just potatoes. The Delgado Plan will work best if you don't smother your vegetables with fatty, oily dressings and cheese.

Vegies and fruits are so low in calories they are actually digested within 15 to 45 minutes (the initial absorption of most of the glucose). This means the next meal should be every 15 to 30 minutes to get sufficient glucose and rarely longer than 90 minutes. You must learn to eat the moment you feel empty, weak, or slightly hungry. That is the signal from your body that your glucose level has begun to drop. The signal to eat will vary by how much and what kind of food you ate at your previous meal or snack. The constant presence of glucose will allow your body to burn fat consistently.

The Krebs cycle is a complex biochemical energy-producing process during which your body must have glucose to burn fat. Glucose is very important to the production of energy. If you don't eat complex carbohydrates to get the precise amount of glucose needed, your body will actually breakdown amino acid (body protein from muscle and organs as a last resort) into glucose to get the necessary amount. Your body cannot convert fat into glucose quick enough to meet the body's needs. This is why foods high in complex carbohydrates are called "protein sparing foods." We spare the protein of the body and from the food, allowing the protein to be used for its special purpose.

Complex carbohydrates should be eaten frequently to protect the body's stores of protein. Don't get the mistaken idea you need protein from meat and cheese when you feel weak (a common misconception). You are only in need of slightly more calories from complex carbohydrates with a greater food density, like grains besides the lighter fruits and vegetables. Eating enough grains, breads, cereal and pastas will give you additional calories, strength and the necessary protein your body requires.

The Delgado Plan allows our bodies to continue to use mostly glucose, along with a constant attack focused on fat in the blood and the storage of fat in the cells.

The quickest way to burn fat is to eat vegetables and fruits approximately every thirty minutes. The frequency between nibbles depends on how you feel, how much activity you're involved with and how big you are. For example, a big, muscular man who is also overweight and doing heavy labor, will need a higher volume of low-fat foods than a small lady, who is slightly overweight, working at a desk. The big man will need more food in his stomach to feel good and get through his workday without undue weakness or fatigue. The smaller woman will feel good eating smaller, less frequent meals. It may not be practical to eat as often as every fifteen to thirty minutes during certain times of the day. If this is the case, then eat more bread, cereals, grains or beans that can sustain you for one to two hours before your next meal.

For example, before a seminar, athletic event or a prolonged business meeting, I eat a bowl of cereal or four slices of bread (two vegetable sandwiches), or one or two bean burritos (without cheese). After the two hours, I return to eating vegetables and fruit for the rest of the day.

Your comfort zone of eating also must be considered. There may be times when you notice it's hard to eat enough fruits and vegetables to feel satisfied. You may start to feel too hungry, weak or bothered by having to eat so often. At that point you should eat grains, breads, pastas, cereals or beans. This will reduce the number of meals you have to eat for convenience sake and will provide a feeling of strength and satisfaction.

Be sure the food you eat has a rich nutritional value. Make calories count! Your body needs fiber, vitamins, minerals, glucose, fat, protein and water. Which food do you think is going to supply these nutritional needs? Liquid diet drinks, which are loaded with sugar, fructose, dairy whey, synthetic chemicals and processed protein? Certainly weight loss is best accomplished eating nature's balanced food supply of fruits, vegetables, grains and legumes that are rich in vitamins, minerals and fiber.

We've become a desperate society bent on self-abuse and denial. People divert their attention from the need to eat properly by blaming the pyschological aspects associated with overeating. Feelings of guilt arise from the resulting appearance of obesity caused by eating fatty foods. This vicious cycle of wanting to punish yourself through starvation for the "sin" of overeating can be broken by simply choosing to eat low-fat, high fiber foods.

Follow the guidelines for the Delgado Program. Forget the out-dated "four food groups" and starvation diets. Reward yourself, don't punish yourself. People don't like to be punished with depleted, poor-tasting starvation drinks. You will be surprised at how great tasting fruits, vegetables and grains can be and what a wonderful reward it will be for you to nibble each hour or two. All people enjoy eating and the Delgado Program will satisfy that powerful urge of hunger. The weight loss you experience will astonish you.

Large servings of potatoes, fruits, vegetables and starches are satisfying foods that fill your stomach's four cup capacity. Compare this to very small servings of fatty foods that concentrate twice as many calories into your stomach. Your stomach sends signals to your brain when it's empty. Your stomach cannot tell the difference in calories; it can only report to the brain when it's empty. By eating frequent meals, eight or more nibblings per day, you will not have as much of a desire for sweets or fatty foods. You will gradually recondition yourself into this new way of eating on the Delgado Plan and become lean and fit for life.

The body panics when food isn't provided regularly and often "saves" calories by storing them as fat. Studies on food intake have shown you will lose weight more easily if you spread 1500 calories over eight or more meals per day, as compared to only three meals or less. Fewer calories are stored as fat when you nibble all day as compared to eating the same food consumed three times per day. Fasting, skipping meals or eating only 1 meal a day puts your body into a panic, increasing the output of certain hormones that encourage fat storage (adipocyte enzyme activity). You can control your body by eating when your stomach feels slightly empty, and you feel weak or hungry. Don't ever wait to eat until you're starved.

In the Oct. 5, 1989, New England Journal of Medicine, David Jenkins, M.D., and associates proved the superiority of the Delgado way of frequent nibbling. People were given seventeen snacks a day, as compared to gorging on three meals per day on the same food. Several metabolic advantages were shown: the "frequent nibblers" experienced a significant reduction in cholesterol by as much as 10%, a 15% reduction in the "bad" LDL cholesterol, 30% less serum insulin output and 20% less output of C-peptide and cortisol in the urine. They also found the most effective diet in controlling lipids was the high carbohydrate, high fiber, low-fat diet with 70% carbohydrate, 15% protein and 15% fat. In two weeks, the Delgado type of program lowered cholesterol down to an average of 189 mg. People eating three meals a day from the four food groups averaged a level of 244. This fattening Weight Watchers type diet is 33% fat, 15% protein and only 52% carbohydrate.

Increased meal frequency, with low-fat, high fiber foods can reduce the rate of obesity in children and in adults. Stop discouraging your children from eating between meals and telling them it will spoil their dinner. We encourage you and your children to eat between meals. We want to stop the bad habit of eating three big meals per day and start eating lighter, more frequent meals. It won't work to eat candy, potato chips and soda pop between meals. Have bowls of cold fruit and vegies cut up in the refrigerator for the family. Each member of the family also should carry a food sack that we call the Delgado Cool Tote - (see next section) to work or school and nibble between breaks. The whole family can stay healthy, fit and trim.

2

THE DELGADO COOL TOTE

M ost people who are unable to maintain high energy or lose weight rely on fatty foods, without fiber. Great health begins with selecting high energy, lowfat foods. This idea will save you money and time as you lose weight and improve your health in the process. Almost every person following the Delgado Health Plan who has tried this easy technique described in this chapter has reported fantastic results within weeks. Are you interested? Consider the following:

When you go to work or leave your home for more than a few hours, there is a tendency to eat whatever is available - candy, doughnuts, fast burgers and fries. As protection from fats and sugars, I would like to tell you about the Delgado Cool Tote.

Every busy person will benefit from this simple idea if used daily. Let me explain how this works: Get yourself an insulated bag with blue ice (Delgado Cool Tote) designed to carry food. Then, once every three days (twice a week) go to the biggest produce market in your area, and buy a selection of your favorite vegies, fruits and breads. Take the Delgado Cool Tote with you wherever you go (especially to work and keep it under your desk). You can nibble on lowfat foods when you feel weak, empty or hungry.

The Delgado Cool Tote idea allows and encourages frequent snacks between meals. Frequent eating from the Cool Tote to overcome hunger, overeating and binging may sound like a contradiction; however, it is actually an easy solution. In a recent poll, it was shown most people snack on extremely high fat foods (ice cream, potato chips, doughnuts, candy and sodas) between or after meals. Our approach - eating tasty, low-fat foods all day long - will protect you from giving in to eating the wrong foods.

I have been training and educating busy people to follow a low-fat, nutritional program since 1978. I found many ways to help people to comply with and follow the program, but none as effective or long lasting as the Delgado Cool Tote. For three years I helped thousands of people to follow the plan, while I only told a handful of people about my special Cool Tote idea.

It was in early 1979 that I hired Bea (Delgado) Campbell (my mother), as a health educator. She spent countless hours with me learning the ideas, teaching students and working with me to help participants follow the program. By the end of 1979, I hired several health educators. I noticed they always followed the program better than anyone else, because they were required to prepare the foods for our food demonstration classes for as many as forty to one hundred people. The educators had to make five-course meals complete with soups, salads, whole grain breads, main dish casseroles and desserts at least four times a week. They were encouraged to eat the unopened, unused leftovers. They followed the low-fat diet perfectly because it was the only food they had in their refrigerator and kitchen. I also noticed the educators began carrying their foods with them in ice chests or sacks, as I had been doing for years, to guarantee the right food was eaten at all times.

The Delgado Cool Tote should contain your favorite types of fruits, vegetables and breads you enjoy eating. The average food sack filled with fruits and vegetables weighs about ten to fifteen pounds. If you want to lose weight, purchase those foods that are low in calories.

Buy vegetables that are easy to carry: a basket of cherry tomatoes, yellow or red bell peppers, etc. Eat the peppers raw and you will be surprised how refreshing and crisp they taste.

Red bell peppers are four times higher in Vitamin C than oranges, and green peppers are twice as high. White corn and yellow corn in the husk can be peeled and surprisingly, tastes mildly sweet when eaten raw. Take along one or two carrots and a small stalk of celery.

I also get vegetables in a jar like new potatoes (which are small, bite-size, and already cooked), green string beans and green peas. I take a spoon with me, pour off the juice and just eat the peas, potatoes or string beans right from the jar. Chinese snow peas are delicious eaten raw so take enough to last a few days.

You can microwave vegetables in the morning. Pour salsa, low- sodium Worcestershire Sauce or mustard on them, take a fork in your tote and and eat them on the way to work. Many of our participants put cooked potatoes - red, rose or white - in a baggy to be eaten during the day from their Cool Tote. It's best to remove the skin from the potato. The green substance under the skin called solanine has been known to cause liver problems when consumed in excess. You can microwave your vegies at work if you prefer. However, many busy people have to eat on the go and save themselves time by taking a bite of potato or fruit at a stop light on the way to and from work.

You should purchase enough vegetables and fruit to last about three days. Some fruits take two to three days to ripen. Leave unripened fruit at home in a bag to ripen. When they are ready to eat, take them with you in your Cool Tote. A ready supply of fruit for your Cool Tote can help reduce the number of visits you need to make to the market.

Your Cool Tote would be complete if you make sure there is a variety of fresh fruit. Favorite selections for your tote can include Rainer cherries (yellow), grapes, pears, plums, peaches and bananas. Bananas can be eaten daily on our weight loss plan because they have less than 2% fat and are relatively low in calories per volume. Eat fresh apples, nectarines, blueberries, blackberries and raspberries. Frozen berries can be placed in a lid-tight container and eaten as they thaw during the day. The best way to design your Cool Tote contents would be to carry a variety of each fruit, and snack from whichever item your heart desires at the moment.

People who are accustomed to starvation diets, calorie restriction and skipping meals will be afraid to try this. However, you will find yourself several pounds lighter in six months without any deprivation, weakness or danger associated with those old ways of dieting.

The Delgado Plan will work for compulsive eaters, busy people and all for whom diet plans have failed. Your food bill probably will drop dramatically, since you will reduce your expenditures on prepared foods. Also, you may find yourself skipping routine restaurants stops. Most of my busy participants (Delgado seminar graduates and patients) go to restaurants for variety or for special occasions. As you reduce the frequent restaurant trips, you can save literally hundreds of dollars. On those occasions when you do go to a restaurant, be sure to nibble from your Delgado Cool Tote in the car on your way to the restaurant. By doing so, you will find yourself ordering less or no fatty foods from the menu.

If you're in the car for long periods or going to be in warm weather, you should invest in the Delgado Cool Tote. Our Cool Tote (insulated bag with blue ice), is available by mail order. If you wish, you may charge it to your credit card and have it sent to your home UPS or pick one up at our office. (The large tote has a strap so you can carry it and your briefcase, leaving a free hand to open doors, etc.) The tote also comes with a blue ice packet to keep your fruits and vegies cold. You should freeze the ice packet every night and put it back in your tote every morning. If you travel and you don't have access to a refrigerator-freezer, just put ice in a plastic ziplock bag with the blue ice. Place the bag upright in the tote and at the end of the day, drain the water and add new ice cubes. The Delgado Cool Tote provides an easier, safer method of food transport. We cover the ice with one or two paper towels to absorb the small amount of moisture from the condensed water. At night when you get home from work, put the vegies and fruit into the refrigerator crisper. Leave them in the bag so you can just put them in your Cool Tote without delay. You must plan to carry your Cool Tote with you every day. Don't forget to assemble your foods in time for work the next day.

It will be necessary to keep your Cool Tote with you, at your work station. If you are unable to keep your tote near you, then take a banana, apple or some bread to nibble. If your food is left in the refrigerator, you may not get the chance to snack when your body signals hunger. You may get distracted by your busy work schedule, and when you finally do eat, you'll be ravenous. You'll eat that doughnut, chocolate, cheese or potato chips that add fat. Just pinch yourself on your hips or waist! RIGHT?!

Nibble every thirty minutes to an hour if you're eating fruits and vegies to lose weight. When eating more grains, breads, beans and casserole dishes, you'll find you only need to eat every two hours. Remember, grains and beans will sustain you longer since they are lower in water content than fruits and vegetables and are more concentrated in food substance. We encourage you to have a whole grain bread in your Cool Tote and eat at least two to four slices a day. You also need the high fiber, vitamins and minerals that grains provide for long-term good health.

Eat from your Cool Tote right up to the time you're going to eat at a restaurant or go home for lunch or dinner. You will be able to maintain control and select foods properly at these traditional set meal times. You may find you won't need to stop for lunch or dinner and many days you'll just eat straight from your tote. Consider the time it will save. Time that can be allocated for a family walk, swim or outings to the park, beach or movies (take your Cool Tote!) You can read to your children, or take turns exercising on mini-trampolines and stationary bikes while you watch TV. Besides the suggested snacking, we encourage you to have family meals together. Your family will benefit as they enjoy improved health and fitness on the Delgado Plan.

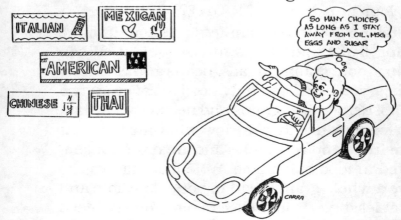

3

TEN RULES FOR FAST FAT LOSS

In the United States today, obesity effects more than 70 million Americans, and taken as a whole, we carry around 2.3 billion pounds excess body fat! To acheive Optimum Weight Control, we must choose a high-carbohydrate, lowfat, high-fiber diet combined with a consistent exercise program. Let's first discuss our diet as compared to those of other countries.

In our country, only 22% of our diet is composed of complex carbohydrates (unprocessed whole grains, beans, fruits and vegetables), and as a result, over 32% of our people are obese. In countries such as Uruguay and Venezuela where they eat a diet higher (53-60%) in fiber and starchy complex carbohydrates, only 20% of the people are overweight. Yet when you examine countries where the diet is composed of over 70-80% complex carbohydrates, obesity is almost nonexistent.

The FIRST RULE for weight loss is simple: The more complex carbohydrates (potatoes, fruit, vegetables, salads, pastas, brown rice, etc.) you eat, the more likely you'll have an ideal body weight.

THE SECOND RULE is to eat large amounts of soups because they are filling and satisfying. Make very thick, flavorful vegetable soups and you will lose fat weight quickly, without being hungry.

The THIRD RULE would be to keep several containers of chopped vegetables in your refrigerator. These vegetables can be used to make large salads and casseroles. When you begin using a large serving bowl in place of a small, standard size bowl, you will be eating your way to a more slender body!

The FOURTH RULE is to eat more fruit, because fruit (like vegetables) is high in water content and high in fiber, both of which have almost no calories. Even bananas are a good weight loss food (along with melon, pears, nectarines, oranges, etc.) You will lose fat if you snack on fruit and vegetables constantly, day and night, with meals or between meals. If you have a sweet tooth and you have trouble resisting fatty candy bars, then you can eat fruit like cherries, blueberries, grapes and watermelon in place of those sweets. You will still get those cravings for candy; however, if you have a ready supply of fruit to eat at all times, then you can successfully resist temptations.

The FIFTH RULE of weight control is by reducing fat, you reduce calories. Every gram of fat has 9 calories. Yet every gram of carbohydrate or protein provides just 4 calories. Remember, fats have 2 1/4 times more calories, which is why they're called "fats" and why they are so "fattening.'' Read labels on the foods you buy to be sure you're eating less than 45 grams of fat per day. On a 2,000 calorie diet this works out to be 20% fat; on a 1,000 calorie weight loss diet, you should eat less than 22 grams of fat daily. Generally, a food should contain less than 4 grams of fat per one cup serving. You must limit or avoid fats, oils, margarine, eggs, lowfat and whole milk, cheese, peanut butter and fatty meats.

The SIXTH RULE to weight control is to be sure to eat more foods high in fiber and low in food density. Your stomach can hold about four cups of food before a signal is sent to the brain that tells you that you're full. If you begin eating large amounts of complex carbohydrates that are naturally high in fiber, most of the food you eat will be low in food density and very low in calories. This is because fiber by definition is non-digestible. Because you can't digest fiber for calories, it just passes out of the body. So, if you ate four cups of food for breakfast (cooked oatmeal or cracked wheat with bran and fruit), four cups of food for lunch (salad bar of vegetables and fruit, sandwich of whole wheat bread with vegies or beans inside), and four cups of dinner (salad bar, soup, fruit, potato, corn and Spanish brown rice), with light snacks of vegies and fruit between meals, your stomach capacity would be fully satisfied throughout the day.

The best thing is even with all this tasty food, you would have only consumed about 900 to 1200 calories for the day! This would allow you to lose weight at a safe and healthful pace, free of hunger.

Always ask yourself these questions: Does this food contain fiber? Is it of plant origin? Is it unprocessed? For example, do cheese, steak, chicken, fish, milk, yogurt, eggs, hamburgers, mayonnaise or vegetable oil have fiber in them? The answer is no. Foods of animal origin have no fiber. They are totally digested and absorbed as calories. Foods like sugar and vegetable oil have lost their fiber through man-made processing. One of the worst examples of man's intervention into Mother Nature's food supply is corn oil. We waste over 14 ears of corn to make 1 tablespoon of oil!

Dr. Denis Burkitt was able to show the importance of eating foods high in fiber in his study of 23 young Irishmen. They were told to eat 2 lbs. of potatoes (about 10 large potatoes) every day for three months. Since they ate their daily ration of potatoes, they were allowed to add as many other foods as they wanted. After the study, every man had lost weight. The 4-cup capacity of the stomach was filled after eating three or four of the large potatoes, and there wasn't much room for other high calorie foods. In fact, 2 lbs. of potatoes have only 690 calories, and a cup of potatoes has just 115 calories. Yet one cup of french fries contains 450 calories! A cup of so-called "lean" hamburger labeled 21% fat would have over 750 calories. A cup of sugar has nearly 800 calories, while the original sugar beet, with its fiber intact, has only 54 calories. And while a cup of corn has only 137 calories, a cup of corn oil has a whopping 1,927 calories or 120 calories per tablespoon.

WEIGHT LOSS GUIDE
by Food Density, Fiber and calories
(Number of calories per 8 oz.)
Low density, fiberous foods
UNLIMITED USE for weight loss

10 Lettuce
16 Cucumbers
20 Celery/Mushrooms
24 Cabbage/Bok Choy
28 Cauliflower/Squash (summer)
31 Turnip greens/Green beans
32 Mustard greens
33 Bell peppers (green)
36 Asparagus
40 Broccoli/Spinach
45 Tomatoes
46 Carrots
47 Bell peppers (red)
54 Brussels sprouts/Beets
64 Artichokes
70 Grapes/Peaches
70 Gazpacho soup
73 Apples
79 Apricots

81 Oranges/Pineapple
93 Squash (winter)
101 Pears
109 Peas (green)
118 Potatoes

Medium density, fibrous food
MEDIUM USE

125 Corn grits
132 Oatmeal
137 Corn
191 Bananas
195 Bread (whole)

High density, high fiber foods
MODERATE USE

224 Beans: lentil, pinto, kidney, etc.
232 Brown rice
291 Sweet potatoes

High density, low fiber foods
OCCASIONAL USE (High calorie
or cholesterol)

88 Skim milk
117 Apple juice
124 Yogurt (skim)/Egg whites
125 Cottage cheese (uncreamed)
145 Lowfat milk
148 Shrimp
170 Clams
188 Oysters
218 Fish, halibut
232 Chicken (no skin)
234 Soybeans
246 Turkey
250 Liteline cheese

384 Avocados
430 Flank steak
799 Cashews/Walnuts/Pecans/Sunflower seeds
849 Almonds

High density, no fiber foods
RESTRICT/AVOID (High fat or cholesterol)

159 Milk (whole)
222 Eggs
342 Ice cream
345 Evaporated milk
420 McDonald's Quarter Pounder
450 Cheddar cheese
750 Hamburger meat patty (21% fat)
667 Chocolate
770 Sugar (white)
794 Maple syrup
821 Sugar (brown)
1520 Peanut butter
1625 Butter
1634 Margarine
1927 Corn oil

Beans, grains and cereals are a great source of fiber, however, these foods are high in food density and higher in calories. So eat grains, brown rice, whole wheat bread and beans in small portions - after eating foods that are low in food density like fruits, vegies and soups. (Up to four cup servings of grains per day.) Also, to lose weight when you do eat grains, you should eat hot, cooked cereals (cracked wheat, oatmeal, 4-grain, etc.) or puffed cereals for breakfast, as opposed to flakes or granola cereals. Cooking cereal with water will cause 1/3 cup to enlarge to fill the whole bowl. Flakes and granola cereals have more calories because they are heavier and concentrated in food density. Puffed cereals are lighter in food density, which makes them a good choice for weight loss. You may include wheat bran in your diet to speed food through your digestive tract so you can absorb fewer calories and lose weight faster.

The SEVENTH RULE is to reduce sugar consumption, and to substitute whole fruit (pineapple, strawberries, etc.) for sugar wherever possible. Sugar causes your body to release too much insulin, which can cause reactive hypoglycemia. This makes you extremely hungry, a condition to avoid when dieting! Also, insulin promotes additional fat storage throughout your body. Use apple butter or apple juice concentrate, but use them in small amounts to avoid reactions.

The EIGHTH RULE would be to eat frequent meals or snacks whenever you're hungry - be sure NOT to skip meals. Body fat is burned most efficiently in the presence of carbohydrates and burning the fat properly is comparable to making a fire with the proper wood. Eating meals high in complex carbohydrates regularly also will "spare" body proteins, organs and muscles from being used as fuel. The body prefers to burn glucose from carbohydrates. So don't skip meals, or you will lose body proteins that can be converted to glucose more easily than body fat.

The NINTH RULE is to exercise consistently and properly for maximum weight loss. Recent experiments have shown exercises involving the largest muscle groups (legs, hips and back), such as walking, jogging, dancing, using mini-trampolines, stairsteppers, treadmills and exercise bikes, will burn off more fat from the hard-to-lose areas like the stomach, thighs or hips, than will specific exercises like sit-ups and bending motions.

In one important experiment, 13 college men completed 5,004 sit-ups during a 27-day program, averaging about 187 sit-ups daily per person. Each man's fat content was measured both by fat biopsies and water immersion. As we suspected, there was no greater fat loss in the abdominal fat cells than in the fat storage in cells located throughout the body. This means spot reducing (sit-ups or arm exercises) will tone up specific muscles, but will not reduce fat cells in specific areas. So, the best way to burn fat is to do exercises using the largest muscle groups because more total calories will be burned up in a given amount of time.

To burn off the most fat from your stomach, hips or whichever part you're trying to reduce, you should walk, jog, dance, etc. continuously for at least 15 to 60 minutes a day. Although the stomach muscles are too small a group to get maximum fat burning, you should still do toning exercises for all specific muscle groups to keep firm. In addition, it's been found exercising about 30 minutes just before your evening meal will help to reduce your appetite by releasing glycogen (storage glucose). This will help you to burn more fat weight and maintain muscle tone. However, the best time to exercise for most people is in the morning. Studies have shown long term adherence to an exercise plan is better for morning exercisers as compared with evening exercisers.

DELGADO EXERCISE FOR FITNESS AND FAT LOSS

15-60 minutes per day, 5-6 days a week: Aerobic walking with Heavy hands, stairstepper. Jogging, stationary biking for long, slow distances.

20 minutes, 2 days a week: Light weight lifting for muscle toning.

The TENTH RULE is to remain patient. Don't be discouraged with seemingly slow weight loss. If you had been on a high protein diet, your tissues would have been dehydrated. As you follow the Delgado Health Plan, your muscles will reabsorb vital fluid. Also your body will hold 4 to 10 lbs. more bulk food in the intestines. You may believe you're gaining weight during the first month following the program. Actually, you'll be burning fat at the most rapid pace of any program yet developed. Stay on the Delgado Plan at least six months, and you will appreciate how easily those inches of fat will shrink away, without being hungry. Calorie and portion restricted programs leave you hungry, but on the Delgado Plan you can eat tasty, lowfat foods whenever you feel slightly empty or hungry. You will always feel good, month after month, which is strong motivation to stay on this plan for life.

Men tend to carry fat weight around the waist area. Women retain fat mostly in the hips, thighs and buttocks. This is a genetic problem that will take about six months to two years to resolve on the best possible program, the Delgado Health Plan. Fat can take a few years to get rid of, which is why you must establish this plan as a way of life. When you lose the fat, you can keep it off for a lifetime. Listen to cassette tapes daily for long term motivation, support and instructions. Feeding your mind with positive thoughts will help you to keep on track and achieve your weight loss goal.

TEN RULES FOR FAT LOSS SUMMARY
1. Eat more complex carbohydrates.
2. Eat large bowls of soup several times per day.
3. Eat large servings of vegies for lunch,

snacks and dinner - salad bar, soups or casseroles.
4. Eat whole fresh fruit (3-8 pieces per day).
5. Reduce fats to less than 22 grams per day.
6. Eat high fiber, low density foods.
7. Reduce sugar (simple carbohydrates).
8. Eat frequent meals whenever you are slightly hungry.
9. Exercise daily (15 to 60 minutes): do aerobics, walk, or jog, etc.
10. Be patient: expect great results in six months to two years.

Follow the ten rules listed above and you will attain your ideal weight. After you've achieved your perfect weight, be sure to switch to our weight maintenance program. (Increase your intake of grains, beans, sweet potatoes, breads, uncooked cereals, and reduce the use of vegetables, fruits and wheat bran.) We also suggest you see our nutritionists to monitor your progress.

SELECTION OF FOODS FOR FAT LOSS

EAT OR SNACK (EVERY 1/2 HOUR TO 2 HOURS) WHEN YOU FEEL WEAK, EMPTY OR MILDLY HUNGRY. IF YOU ARE NOT MILDLY HUNGRY OR WEAK, THERE IS NO NEED TO EAT AT THAT TIME. WAIT FOR YOUR BODY'S SIGNAL TO EAT. EAT AS MUCH AS YOU WANT

UNTIL SATISFIED OF SOUPS, VEGIES, FRUIT BELOW:

SOUPS: broths, vegetable, tomato (no milk).

VEGIES: cucumbers, cauliflower, tomatoes, broccoli, cabbage, squash, snow peas, potatoes, carrots, mushrooms, bell peppers, bean sprouts, seed sprouts, grain sprouts, etc.; vegetable casserole, salads.

FRUIT: melon, oranges, grapes, apples, pears, berries, bananas, plums, cherries, nectarines, etc.

LOW DENSITY GRAINS: hot air popcorn, rice cakes, puffed cereal, cooked oat bran cereal.

DESSERT: sorbet, strawberry icee, frozen banana.

FIBER: psyllium husk, wheat bran, corn bran, oat bran.

SPICES: garlic, chili, pepper, dill, onion, cilantro, etc.; non-fat salad dressing, mustard, catsup, vinegar.

HERB TEAS: camomile, red bush, chinese, linden.

BEVERAGES: mineral water, Sundance fruit drink, 2-4 glasses water per day, tomato juice, carrot juice; grain drinks: Caffix, Postum, Carob.

RESTAURANT DINING - FILL UP ON SOUP & SALADS. ADD ONE PLATEFUL OF A

MAIN DISH SELECTION LISTED BELOW:

AMERICAN: soup and salad bars, fruit, baked potato, hash browns (dry), Egg Beaters or egg whites (no cheese).

DELI: whole wheat sandwich w/lettuce, tomato, vinegar, pepper, bell peppers, onion, mustard, no oil.

CHINESE: (order no oil, no MSG, no egg) mixed vegetables, chop suey, broccoli, snow peas, vegetable soup, hot & sour soup (no pork), vegetable chow mein, moo-shu (no meat), steamed rice.

JAPANESE: (sushi-California roll (no fish eggs), cucumber roll, miso soup, cucumber salad, noodles.)

MEXICAN: steamed corn tortillas, lettuce, tomato, salsa, gazpacho soup, tortilla soup (no cheese), black bean soup, lentil soup, cocido (vegetable), tostada, burrito, vegie taco (no cheese), beans, rice, salsa.

ITALIAN: green salad, minestrone soup, steamed mushrooms, zucchini, cheeseless pizza (w/mushrooms, bell pepper, pineapple, tomato), pasta with "fat free" tomato sauce (no oil, no meat, no cheese), sourdough bread.

**EAT SMALL PORTIONS,
LIMIT TO 2 TO 4 CUPS PER DAY:**

GRAINS: cooked cereals (cracked wheat,

oatmeal, 4-grain, etc.), cereal flakes, granolas, museli, brown rice, millet, whole wheat pastas, wheat meat.

BREADS: whole wheat or corn tortillas, Essene or Manna sprouted bread, whole wheat pretzels, crackers (low-fat), oat bran muffins (no yolk).

LEGUMES: beans (pinto, black, navy, lentil), black-eyed peas, tostada or burrito (no cheese), hummus, garbanzo.

VEGETABLES: yams, sweet potatoes.

DESSERTS: fruit pie (whole wheat crust, no sugar), whole wheat or oatmeal cookies (low-fat, no sugar)

BEVERAGES: Amazake rice milk, fruit smoothies.

FOODS TO AVOID OR LIMIT (AS NOTED)
HIGH FAT OR HIGH SUGAR FOODS - LIMIT TO 1-2 OUNCES PER DAY:

NUTS/SEEDS: almonds, cashews, pecans, nut butter, sunflower seeds, sesame seeds.

SNACKS: potato chips, corn chips, crackers.

MISC.: soybeans, soy cheese, tofu, avocado, olives, coconut, rice bran.

SWEETS: Rice Dream (non-dairy ice cream), raisins, dates, apple butter, pancake syrup, jams and jellies (unsweetened), angel food cake.

SAUCES/ SPICES: A-1, Worcestershire (vegetable-based), barbeque sauce, Molly McButter or Butter Buds.

HIGH PROTEIN FOODS - LIMIT TO 1 OUNCE PER DAY OR AVOID:

DAIRY: lowfat cheese (Lifetime, Liteline, Dorman's, Weight Watcher's), nonfat milk, nonfat yogurt.

LEAN FISH: halibut, sole, scallops, clams, sushi.

CRUSTACEA: shrimp, crab, lobster.

LEAN MEAT: chicken, turkey, range-fed beef, flank steak, Canadian bacon, fat-reduced ham, lamb.

HIGH SUGAR OR CAFFEINE - LIMIT TO 4 OUNCES (4 CUPS) PER WEEK OR AVOID:

BEVERAGES: soda pop, diet drinks, alcohol, coffee, tea.

SUGARS, SALT - LIMIT TO 1/3 TSP. PER DAY OR AVOID:

SUGARS: sugar, fructose, chocolate syrup, sugar cereals, artificial sweeteners.

SPICES: salt, garlic salt, soy sauce, Accent (M.S.G.).

HIGH CHOLESTEROL, HIGH FAT - AVOID:

EGGS: egg yolks, products with whole eggs added, caviar.

FATS: butter, margarine, lard, vegetable oil, olive oil, corn oil, canola oil, fish oil, cod oil, etc.; mayonnaise, nondairy creamers, oily or creamy dressings.

DAIRY: cheese (jack, mozzarella, cheddar, Swiss, etc.) cream, ice cream, yogurt, whole milk, powdered milk.

SWEETS: chocolate candy, cake, cookies.

MEAT: steak, ham, bacon, pork, sausage, salmon, organ meats, liver, hot dogs (beef, chicken or turkey franks), bologna, etc.

SAMPLE "FAST" FAT LOSS MEAL PLAN
DAY ONE

BREAKFAST: Bowl hot cereal (oatmeal, wheat, 4-grain or 7-grain with peaches, pears or prunes and 2 tbls. wheat bran.

SNACK: Fruit and vegetables.

LUNCH: 1 large bowl vegie salad w/non-fat dressing, 2 fruits.

SNACK: Potato, herb tea.

DINNER: Chinese restaurant - vegies, chop suey, broccoli, mushrooms, cabbage,(NO MSG, NO OIL), add spicy szechuan.

DAY TWO

BREAKFAST: Oatbran cereal cooked in 1/2 apple juice & 1/2 water, 1/4 cantaloupe.

SNACK: Vegetable, water w/3 tbls. psyllium husk.

LUNCH: Minestrone soup, 2 fruits, baked potato w/salsa.

SNACK: Green peas, tomato juice.

DINNER: Cheeseless pizza w/mushrooms, tomatoes, peppers.

DAY THREE

BREAKFAST: Potatoes (microwave - cover with glass bowl), mixed vegies, soup.

SNACK: Tomatoes, corn, peas.

LUNCH: Vegetable soup, salad, fruit.

SNACK: Banana, grapes, nectarine.

DINNER: Potato pancakes, vegies, soup, fruit, frozen banana ice cream.

DAY FOUR

BREAKFAST: Whole grain muffins w/apple butter, fruit.

SNACK: 1 slice bread, tomatoes.

LUNCH: Vegie sandwich: cucumbers, cauliflower, tomato, artichoke hearts (packed in water), mustard, barbeque sauce.

SNACK: Fruit, carrot juice.

DINNER: Mixed vegies casserole, soup, fruit, baked potato with ketchup or Molly McButter.

DAY FIVE

BREAKFAST: Puffed cereal with added two

tablespoons wheat bran, use Amazake rice milk, water or juice, fruit.

SNACK: Fruit.

LUNCH: Vegie taco (soft corn tortillas, salsa, lettuce, sprouts, mushrooms, tomato, potato), cabbage soup.

SNACK: 1 bread roll, mineral water with lemon or cherry flavor.

DINNER: Vegies, soup, fruit, Nouvelle Sorbet ice cream.

NOTE:

If you have to leave home to go to work, be sure to take your Delgado Cool Tote (filled with your favorite fruits, vegetables and bread) to nibble from during the day.

For good nutrition be sure to eat the following daily:

Two different types of whole grains, at least 1 citrus fruit, 1 green vegetable, 1 yellow vegetable and a small serving of beans or peas in a soup or salad and a supplemental source of Vitamin B12 or foods like cereals fortified with B12.

Repeat any breakfast, lunch or dinner you like. Keep it simple and convenient. Eat until you feel satisfied. Don't let yourself get weak or hungry by not eating.

4
EATING AT HOME OR RESTAURANTS

At home you can prepare meals centered on several high complex carbohydrate dishes, with vegetables, salads, soups and fruit ice creams for dessert.

Microwave cooking is great for busy people. Look for pre-packaged, microwave-ready fresh vegetables that include squash, potatoes, broccoli, snow peas and carrots. Try potato pancakes (Manischewitz) that can be poured directly from the package into a Pyrex bowl. Mix with filtered or bottled water and cook for three minutes in the microwave. Eat them like you would mashed potatoes. Potato pancakes have a spicy, onion flavor and taste great without being fried. The sodium content is high (1400 mg per serving) so if you're on a sodium restricted diet, then limit the use of these pancakes to twice a week. Almost every big grocery store I've been to has these pancakes in the Jewish food section next to Matzo balls.

Frozen vegetables without oils, butter, sauces or salt are convenient and easy to prepare for busy people who want to lose weight fast. Brussel sprouts, broccoli, cauliflower, lima beans or green peas are favorites with a three minute average cooking time. Blend with a dash of mustard, salsa and Worcestershire Sauce or you may want to try all three condiments in different corners of the vegetable container. We suggest you try a variety of mustards: Dijon, garlic, or jalepeno. Try catsup from the health food store or diet section of the market without added sugar. Use chili salsas: red, green or mixed, or blends like Pace, Ortega, Rosarita and La Victoria (mild, medium or hot) on potatoes or vegetables. They're great! Barbeque sauce without sugar can be obtained at specialty stores, health food stores and at Delgado Medical.

Weight control can begin with breakfast, because that is how most people start out the day. If you want to drop fat weight fast, you might begin your morning with just fruit, vegetables or a soup. The ideal type of cereal for weight loss is a hot cooked cereal, because when you cook the grain (cracked wheat, old-fashioned rolled oats, 4-grain cereal, etc.), the cereal absorbs much of the water that fills up the bowl and reduces the density of food concentration. The best hot cooked cereal for weight loss is oat bran cereal, since bran, by its very nature, is mostly non-digestible. Most of it passes through your system undigested. As a result, you feel full and satisfied while only absorbing a fraction of the 110 calories for one serving.

Maybe you would like to try puffed rice, wheat or kashi. Since puffed cereals are light and filled with air, the food density will provide fewer calories.

I encourage people to use water or diluted juice with cereals instead of milk to reduce food calorie concentration further and to lessen the potential of food allergy reaction caused by milk (bloating, diarrhea, skin or lung conditions). Milk is a leading cause of food allergies in people throughout the world. You might like Amazake brown rice milk from the health food store. It's sweet and thick, and if you dilute it with water, it tastes very much like nonfat milk without causing allergic reactions. You may want to try cold bottled or filtered water mixed with a small amount of fruit juice (apple, berry, etc.).

It's okay to mix in your favorite fruit with cereal. Don't be afraid of food combining (fruit with a starch). There is no medical evidence to prove the out-dated, mistaken belief about digestive juices being unable to handle food combinations. Even Harvey Diamond in "Fit for Life" was unable to show any substantial evidence on this point. I am convinced the reason this myth was started was because people usually use milk in their cereal. Despite whether fruit is added or not, even the small amount of milk added to cereal may cause an upset stomach, bloating, gas, etc. Some people confused this reaction to be caused by the combination of fruit and cereal.

You will find that cereal and fruit with water or juice is actually tasty. I know the thought of water in cereal may seem strange, but if you'll just try it, I believe, like most people, that you'll grow to prefer it. If you or your children want to maintain or gain weight, you should be serving high-density grain cereals. Muselix, granola (without oil), Nutrigrain, Nutty Rice and other whole grain cereals can be eaten with cold water, juice or rice milk. Growing children need to eat more cereals that provide more calories. My children have for some time enjoyed their old-fashioned rolled oats (raw, uncooked) mixed with Nutrigrain nuggets and water. Try using "No Sugar" Strawberry or Blueberry syrup, or a jam preserve without sugar for added flavor.

At restaurants you can order puffed rice and water with fruit. One of my favorites is Egg Beaters scrambled with mushrooms, tomatoes, bell pepper and chili salsa into an omelette. If they don't offer Egg Beaters, which is low in fat and cholesterol, you can simply order egg whites scrambled without the yolks. I always have one or two orders of dry hash browns (cooked without oil). At a restaurant I'll use the catsup, A-1 sauce or salsa. At home I'll use catsup without added sugar or salt that I purchase from the health food store.

Muffins can be a good choice for a simple meal or snack if they are low in fat. Try an oat bran muffin (made without egg yolk or milk) from speciality stores or homemade from our recipe book.

For lunch or dinner, you might have some microwaveable mixed vegies: potatoes, squash, broccoli or carrots that come in a plastic container. Microwave the vegies for four minutes and use low-sodium Worcestershire Sauce, mustard or salsa. You might even enjoy a hearty vegetable soup that was left over from the weekend pot of soup. You can use a canned soup such as minestrone or Cous Cous cup of soup without oil. Pritikin soup is acceptable; it's just not tasty enough and needs to be spiced up with Mrs. Dash's Spicy Seasoning. If you're trying to lose weight, you need to use soups every day. If not for breakfast, at least lunch and dinner. We have great soup recipes like black bean Cuban, gazpacho, minestrone and potato (without milk).

When eating out, it's true some soups have more sodium than you would normally use (less than 200 mg. of sodium per serving is ideal and not more than 500 mg. is acceptable). However, the vegetable soups are usually so low in fat they make a great filling meal for faster weight loss. If the soup is made with meat (chicken, pork or beef), you should spoon out as much of the meat as possible or when ordering, ask the waitress for less or no meat in your soup. Meat is dense in calories, fat and protein and is without any fiber, so it should only be used as flavoring in food and not as a main dish. Chicken and fish also should be limited to less than a few ounces a week because they have as much cholesterol as red meat! Even if you remove the skin, cholesterol is permeated equally throughout the lean flesh of the chicken or fish.

I love to stop in for a tureen of vegetable soup at Marie Callendar's. Sizzler's, the Soup Exchange and Soup Plantation also have good soups. At a Thai restaurant, I order lemon grass soup extra spicy, which is my absolute favorite. I ask them to substitute broccoli for the large amount of chicken they traditionally use. At Mexican restaurants, I order tortilla soup without cheese, albondigas soup without meatballs, black bean soup without sour cream or gazpacho soup (a cold traditional Spanish soup made with tomatoes, onions and vegetables).

Eat large amounts of salad for rapid weight loss. Restaurants offer salad bars with great selections and be sure to use a low- calorie or non-fat Italian dressing, vinegar or lemon juice. You may even want to try salsa or minestrone soup over your salad! The type of salad dressing that you use on your salads can profoundly influence your goal of weight loss or increased energy. What if you made the mistake of using bleu cheese, thousand island or ranch dressing? This adds as much as 30 to 40 grams of fat, (per three tablespoons of salad dressing) which is as much fat as a typical hamburger!

DINING OUT

Dining out in restaurants takes a bit of finagling and compromise. If you order right off the menu without a special request, you can be sure of getting a high fat, cholesterol, salt or sugar meal. So, to get what you want, you have to ask for what you want!

Dressings and sauces, except tomato sauce, are rich in fat, cholesterol and salt and are easily omitted from most dishes. Whenever possible, ask for your pastas and vegetables to be prepared without butter, margarine or oil. If you have zucchini, mushrooms, carrots or other vegies fried in batter, simply eat the vegetable, avoiding the fried batter.

ITALIAN

Call ahead to ask if they will cook without oil or salt. More restaurants are offering this option.

SALAD: Order a salad with no meat or anchovies. You can have a small amount of Italian dressing (vinegar or lemon juice would be better) and one or two black olives. The peppers and other vegetables are good choices, too.

SOUP: Minestrone is a good choice; most have only small amounts of oil, if any. If you see too much oil, avoid it.

PIZZA: Order your pizza without cheese, and a selection of vegetable toppings. Request extra sauce so the crust doesn't become dry, sprinkle on a little Parmesan. Some pizza parlors offer a whole wheat crust that is preferable.

PASTA: They probably will not have whole wheat pasta, but any pasta, except egg pasta, is okay.

BREAD: Breadsticks or Italian bread are safe. Avoid garlic bread.

VEGETABLES: All vegetables are fine when served without butter, margarine or oil. Try a steamed artichoke or a baked potato with meatless tomato sauce.

FRUIT: A fruit salad or fresh fruit is good for dessert.

CHINESE, JAPANESE OR THAI

When you order, request no oil, eggs, M.S.G., sugar, or soy sauce.

VEGETABLES: Ask them to stir fry your vegetables in chicken or fish stock. They can add cornstarch to thicken and ginger and garlic to flavor. Hot mustard is good to use at the table. Try to select soups and vegetables with broccoli added instead of meat. However, you can have approximately 3 oz. of chicken or fish with your vegetables two or three times per week. Avoid beef, pork and duck. Order chop suey or chow mein with very little oil. For taste variety, try the spicy, hot Szechuan sauces on broccoli, eggplant or other vegetables.

RICE: Choose plain steamed rice instead of fried rice. It is browned by frying in soy sauce or oil. Avoid hors d'oeuvres because they are high in fat and cholesterol.

MEXICAN

Call ahead in the morning to order beans without lard; they may oblige you.

SOUP: Gazpacho, a cold vegetable soup, is good to start the meal. Also, albondigas soup without meatballs or tortilla soup without the cheese.

SALAD: Try a dinner salad with fresh lemon and salsa.

CORN TORTILLAS: Request 1/2 dozen soft and steamed to dip in the salsa. Avoid fried chips. (If they are crispy, they are fried).

ENTREE: Try enchiladas stuffed with rice and no cheese. Try a tostada - ask for a steamed corn tortilla bottom instead of fried. Top with plain beans, shredded lettuce, onion, salsa and just a dab of guacamole.

BURRITOS: Without cheese, add hot sauce to taste.

FRENCH

APPETIZERS: Vegetables in a light vinaigrette, vegetable relish, french bread.

SALADS: Salads of fresh or steamed vegetables, Salad Nicoise without oil or egg yolk may be a safe choice.

ENTREE: Ratatouille (cooked vegetables), a simple vegetable souffle made with egg whites (without the butter), or a baked potato with chives are all tasty choices. Most restaurants will prepare a beautiful steamed vegetable plate to order even if it is not on the menu. Request no salt, butter, margarine, oil or sauces. If your cholesterol level is below 160, you may order broiled fish, chicken (or frog legs) once or twice a week.

AMERICAN
SALAD/SALAD BARS: Fresh vegetables are unlimited. Limit the marinated vegetables, as they may be salted. Request tasty vegetable soups, also try fruit salads. Avoid eggs, meat, excess chicken, turkey, cheese, oil or mayonnaise-based salad dressings, and bacon bits. Try using vinegar or lemon juice with garlic and herbs, if available.

BREAD: Try for whole grain bread or rolls, but if they are not available, anything other than butter or egg bread will do.

ENTREE: Steamed vegetable plate can usually be ordered, even if it is not on the menu. Ask them to omit the butter, oil, margarine, and sauces. A side order of baked potato (request chili salsa instead of butter) or the fresh vegetables of the day can be an excellent main course after the salad bar. You'll leave feeling full, knowing you haven't overstressed your body.

DESSERT: Try fresh fruit or fruit salad. Fruit sorbet is good, too. If you feel very decadent, split a rich dessert among several people - and take tiny bites.

BREAKFAST BONUSES:
- Ask for sugar and salt-free cereals such as oatmeal, Cream of Wheat, Shredded Wheat or Grape-Nuts.
- Order nonfat milk, if available. Otherwise, ask for lowfat milk. Or, better yet, try apple juice with water added instead of milk on cereal!
- Fresh fruit can generally be found at most coffee shops or breakfast houses. Order 1/2 grapefruit, orange sections, melon in season or sliced bananas.
- Always ask for dry toast or rolls, since most restaurants butter your toast for you. If you must, use jam for a spread on toast instead of butter.

LUNCHTIME SAVERS:
- Have hot soup, broth-based instead of creamed, as a main part of your lunch.
- Always order sandwiches on whole grain bread and hold the mayo.

- Look for eating places that offer minimally processed foods. Cafeterias and lunch counters have the advantage of showing you exactly what you are getting. The trick is to choose foods that are not swimming in fat, oil or sugar. Natural and vegetarian restaurants are good choices (The Good Earth, Country Life in Los Angeles, Mother's Kitchen in Huntington Beach, etc.). They offer fresh vegetables and fruit salads, fruits and juices, whole grain breads, vegetable casseroles, etc. Beware of dishes laden with cheese, eggs or oil.
- Try creating your own vegetable sandwich with pita bread or crusty rolls filled with lettuce, tomatoes, pickles, beans, rice, pasta, cucumbers, carrots or cauliflower.
- Pick a fast food restaurant with a salad bar so you can fill up on raw vegetables. Otherwise order the simplest sandwich; leave off the fat-rich hamburger or chicken meat, instead request the bun, lettuce, tomatoes, pickles, mustard, catsup and hold the mayo; eat french fries on a limited basis (surprisingly fries may have less total fat than cheeseburgers or cheese tacos); order fruit juice instead of a milk-shake (fast food restaurants probably will not have nonfat milk). Mashed potatoes (hold the gravy) with several

ears of corn (hold the butter) can be a filling and healthy alternative to chicken.

RESTAURANT DINNER DIVIDENDS:

- Call the restaurant in advance for special requests. This courtesy will improve your chances of getting what you want. The worst that can happen is the restaurant will refuse. In that case, pick another restaurant.
- Eat something before you leave home and nibble from your Delgado Cool Tote in route to the restaurant. It will take the edge off your appetite so that fat laden temptations will not be as difficult to refuse.
- Think before entering. Have a good idea what you will order before you enter a restaurant - then stick to it. Try new dishes only if they fit your basic plan.
- Bank lean meat portions for special occasions.
- Order a la carte to avoid unwanted courses and trimmings.
- Think in terms of lowfat versus high fat choices for each course. For example, if appetizers are placed on the table, concentrate on celery and carrots instead of olives, or for soup, choose hot consomme over cold vichysoise.
- Order meatless dishes or lean meats, such as

fish or poultry instead of fat-marbled red meats. Emphasize vegetables. Choose broiled or baked foods - not fried or french fried.

- Don't be afraid to split a meal with a friend.
- Skip dessert or have fresh fruit in season.
- Doggie bag your leftovers to enjoy the following day.

Remember, BE ASSERTIVE! When it comes to it, your integrity and strength of character will determine if the restaurant is going to serve you and your needs.

SAVING TIME IN THE KITCHEN
SECRETS OF THE PROFESSIONAL CHEF

You come home tired and face the task of preparing dinner for yourself and perhaps your family and friends. Maybe you have an evening engagement, and need to fix something in a hurry.

Certainly convenience foods were made for times like this. But we know what convenience foods contain - usually FAT, SALT AND SUGAR. So what do you do?

Don't give in to processed fast foods. Why not use the techniques of the professional chef, and prepare healthful convenience foods ahead of time to last you a week?

After all, many of us are professionals in our careers. Why shouldn't we apply the same organizational principles to our kitchens and to our health?

PREPARING FOODS FOR THE WEEK
HOW TO DO IT

You will need to set aside a block of time that you can be home, maybe Saturday afternoon, or Sunday, or even Monday evening. You'll probably want to allow a couple of hours. Then get set. The equipment you will need includes:

- A Seal-a-Meal heat sealing device; this costs about $15 at department stores.
- A large stock or soup pan.
- Individual or family-size plastic containers.
- Sauce pans and utensils.
- A food processor is optional.

First, you should wash, peel and cut several kinds of vegetables - the choice is yours. Fill a plastic container with some of them and set another batch aside for making soup.

If you own a microwave, you can prepare vegetables for freezing simply by cooking a dishful for one to two minutes. This "blanches" them, the same as if you had parboiled them.

Next, turn on the oven and throw in several russet potatoes, washed and scrubbed. While you're at it, cook a pot of rice, or a grain mixture. Portion it into Seal-a-Meal bags and freeze, or store in the coldest part of the refrigerator.

Beans help control or reduce cholesterol levels, so now is the time to cook a pot of them. Use three to one proportions of water or chicken stock, add a bay leaf, onion and some garlic.

Make a basic soup or broth. The easiest way is to use Health Valley, Pritikin Unsalted Chicken Stock, or unsalted tomato juice, and add vegetables and herbs.

Here are some extras you might try that take about thirty minutes:

• Make some corn chips out of tortillas, or make wheat chips from chapatis (whole wheat Indian flour tortillas). Slice and place on a cookie sheet, bake at 350 degrees for 10 minutes or until crispy.

USES FOR PRE-COOKED FOODS
PREPARED VEGETABLES

Grab a handful of raw carrots, celery or broccoli for a quick snack. How often have you eaten some "forbidden" high calorie food, when you really wanted something light? Prepare some vegetables ahead of time, and you won't have any more excuses!

You also can take a plastic baggie of vegetables in your Delgado Cool Tote when you leave home and eat them for snacks.

Here are some vegetables you might like to prepare:

• carrot sticks
• celery sticks
• broccoli spears
• zucchini slices
• red, green bell peppers

• jicama sticks
• cauliflower-ettes
• cherry tomatoes
• green onions
• fresh baby green beans

Wash, peel and dry them thoroughly before

storing them in containers. They should be good for two to three days.

SOME VEGETABLES THAT ARE GOOD COOKED AND THEN EATEN COLD:

- artichokes with fresh lemon
- baked yam and sweet potato
- eggplant, cooked and pureed with garlic and basil

BAKED POTATOES CAN BE ENJOYED:

- sliced and diced in soups and casseroles
- grated and cooked in a nonstick pan, or oven-baked with onions as hash browns
- sliced and baked as french fries, or oven-browned potatoes
- sliced and cooked with green onion and green chili salsa (Ortega or homemade) for Mexican-style potatoes
- red and white new potatoes can be cooked, chilled, diced and added to salads

SEITAN'S WHEAT MEAT CAN BE HEATED AND USED IN APPROPRIATE QUANTITIES:

- in sandwiches
- in soups
- as a crepe filling with stir-fried vegetables

BEANS CAN BE USED:

- pureed and served as a bean dip
- in Mexican dishes such as tostadas, chilis and enchiladas

BROWN RICE CAN BE USED IN:
- soups
- casseroles
- pilafs
- stir-fries
- desserts

You can make a pie crust by pressing rice into a pie shell and baking for fifteen minutes; then fill it with vegetable mixture or wheat meat for a delicious pie.

SAMPLE MENUS USING PRE-COOKED FOODS PREPARED ONCE A WEEK

BREAKFASTS:
- Homemade granola with fruits
- Frozen whole wheat waffles or pancakes, with fruit berry topping
- Breakfast burritos
- Breakfast cookie bars

SNACKS:
- Crackers, bread or vegetable sticks with hummus (garbanzo bean dip)
- A pouch of soup, heated in the microwave, or boiled in the bag
- Corn and wheat chips, bean dips and salsa dips

DINNERS:

Wheat meat and vegetable stir-fry made fresh (it only takes fifteen minutes), frozen brown rice, reheated in the microwave, or boiled in the bag

- Banana-ginger freeze
- Spaghetti, served with marinara sauce, tossed green salad, minestrone - frozen, reheated in the pouch
- Tostadas, with lowfat cheese (optional), pre-made bean dip, lettuce, tomatoes, salsa topping

EQUIPPING YOUR KITCHEN

Chances are, if you took a moment to review how your kitchen is set up, you'd wonder how you ever got dinner made. We put up with old pots and pans, cramped quarters and poorly designed preparation areas - conditions we wouldn't tolerate in our professional workspaces. If you take an hour or two to apply the same organizational abilities you use at work to your kitchen, food preparation may even be enjoyable!

THE WORK AREA

Make counter space available, with ample room for cutting. Have a permanent area set up for chopping and get rid of knicknacks and appliances not regularly used. Leave out the equipment you use most often. Knives should be next to the cutting area; spoons and spatulas close to the stove.

ALUMINUM

A growing body of medical evidence points to ingested aluminum involved in the process of

Alzheimer's Disease. That means we should avoid:
- Covering foods directly with aluminum foil, especially acidic foods such as tomato sauce and citrus fruits
- Aluminum pots, pans, tea kettles
- Heating foods packaged in aluminum containers

RECOMMENDED COOKWARE:
- Silverstone - or other "nonstick" cookware
- Stainless steel with copper bottoms
- Porcelain
- Corningware
- Glass
- Iron skillets are excellent because they conduct heat well. But, they also add a significant amount of iron to your diet. Therefore, be careful not to use iron pots daily, unless you're iron deficient as diagnosed by blood test.

A chef's knife is indispensable. Make sure the blade is the right size for your hand. It should balance pleasingly. Nine-inch blades are about right for most women's hands. Stainless steel is easier to care for than carbon steel.

OTHER GREAT TIME SAVING TOOLS
- Microwave ovens
- Food processors with slicing and grating discs

- Salad spinners for drying lettuce, also doubles as a colander or drainer
- Pasta cooker
- "Gravy strainer" or "Soup strainer" - brand name for a clever container that separates fat from liquids
- Rice cooker
- Vegetable steamer
- Wok
- Crockpot

GUIDELINES FOR ADAPTING RECIPES

IF THE RECIPE CALLS FOR:	TRY INSTEAD:
whole eggs	egg substitutes, egg whites
whole milk	nonfat milk, rice milk
mayonnaise	nonfat yogurt, non-dairy low-fat mayo
frying	baking, broiling, frying in nonstick pan, with minimum fat
salt	a blend of herbs and spices
ground beef	wheat meat or extra lean ground beef with grain filler
oil for sauteing	chicken or vegetable broth

mustard	salt-free mustard
steak sauce	Mrs. Dash salt-free steak sauce
ketchup	basic recipe ketchup
baking soda, powder	low sodium baking soda, powder
graham cracker crumbs	low oil granola, ground Grape Nuts in limited quantity
sugar	less sugar, juice concentrates, low sugar jams, apple butter, vanilla, cinnamon, nutmeg, barley malt
cheese	low fat, low sodium cheese

Here is what to use instead of butter or oil in different cooking techniques:

SAUTEING VEGETABLES: Use a little liquid - water, vegetable or chicken broth, in the bottom of a skillet. Bring liquid to a boil, then add vegetables and stir until browned, allowing most of the liquid to evaporate. While sauteing, add extra liquid if vegetables look too dry.

You also can brown vegetables directly in a dry, non-stick skillet. Avoid using a high heat and watch the cooking process carefully to avoid scorching vegetables. This also can be applied to sauteing rice for a pilaf; or use a non-stick pan and oven- toast, watch carefully so the rice will not burn.

FRYING: On stove top, use non-stick skillet without fat to "fry" patties, potato pancakes, French toast, pancakes, etc. Use a non-stick baking sheet without fat to oven-"fry" breaded eggplant, potatoes, vegetables, etc. Some foods lend themselves well to either a skillet on the stove or a baking sheet for oven frying.

MARINADES: Replace oil or fat with compatible liquids: lemon juice, vinegar, vegetable broth or fat-free stock, tomato juice, fruit juice, rice milk, low-salt soy sauce, cooking wines, etc.

BASTING: Use acceptable liquids such as those suggested under Marinades, as well as rendered juices from food being cooked.

SWEETENING TIPS: Fruits and fruit juices are most often required for sweetening. However, there are more subtle ways to sweeten foods. Cooking with carrots is one good way. They can give a sweet flavor to soups and entrees that normally call for a tablespoon or two of sugar, such as spaghetti sauce. If a little sugar is called for in a recipe, try adding a diced or chopped carrot. Or put in large whole carrot to simmer with the sauce, then remove it before serving. If you want to make the recipe even sweeter, add a swig of apple or pineapple juice. You can use carrots to sweeten a navy bean casserole, instead of the usual molasses and brown sugar. Cook the carrots and some apple juice in the bean liquid.

Naturally sweet vegetables like sweet potatoes, squash and yams make great pies and hot casseroles, and when chilled are gooey-sweet snacks. Sweet corn is another vegetable that lends a natural sweetness.

For some types of cooking and baking, to complement the sweetness you are trying to achieve, the flavor of vanilla will help. Use vanilla extract or whole vanilla beans. For chocolate, you can substitute carob powder, but beware of the carob bars sold in health food stores, which generally have sugar and fat additives comparable to a chocolate bar.

Also, use spices to best advantage. Certain spices, such as oregano or peppers, impart a slightly bitter quality, as opposed to sweet basil, for example. Spices such as coriander, cinnamon, nutmeg, allspice, curry, cardamom, ginger and mace tend to complement a sweet flavor. The omission of salt from recipes will also automatically sweeten a dish.

TO MAKE GRAVY FROM FAT-FREE STOCK: Remove all traces of fat from meat, fish or fowl stock by refrigerating or freezing the stock until fat is congealed. Remove fat with a large spoon and pour stock through several thicknesses of cheesecloth to remove remaining fat. You may want to freeze the defatted stock in premeasured amounts or in ice cube trays.

Add to the fat-free stock desired seasoning and other liquids of choice, such as vegetable broth, rice milk or a dash of soy sauce. Then thicken according to the following methods:

THICKENING HINTS: For sauces, stews and many soups (cream-style and others), cornstarch or arrowroot can be used for thickening. Arrowroot clears completely, so it should be used where greater transparency is desirable. While it makes a delicate sauce, it does not reheat well. Cornstarch may leave a little cloudiness, but is preferable for some uses, such as thickening a white sauce, as it gives desirable color. (Arrowroot may be purchased at health or natural food stores).

To use cornstarch or arrowroot, follow these suggestions:

Make a thin paste of the cornstarch or arrowroot in a little cold liquid (water or other acceptable liquid). One level tablespoon of arrowroot will thicken one cup of liquid. Cornstarch has slightly more thickening capacity, so a little less will be needed to thicken the same amount of liquid.

Bring liquid to be thickened to a boil. If using cornstarch, simmer liquid gently as you slowly pour in the paste, stirring as you pour. With arrowroot, remove saucepan from heat as you do this step, then return to heat and again bring to a boil. Stir while liquid thickens.

Flours, such as wheat and potato, are also good thickening agents and can be used instead of cornstarch or arrowroot for some recipes.

For some foods, a thickening agent such as those described is not required to get good results. For example, a spaghetti sauce is preferably thickened by reduction; that is, reducing it to the proper thickness. The sauce is slowly simmered, uncovered, until enough liquid evaporates to produce the desired consistency. This method also works well with soups. Another very handy way to thicken soups like split pea, minestrone, bean or vegetable is to puree a portion of it in the blender, and then return it to the soup pot. With this method, the blended soup vegetables act as a thickener.

INSTEAD OF 1 CUP ALL-PURPOSE WHITE FLOUR

1/2 cup barley flour
3/4 cup coarse whole wheat flour
3/4 cup barley flour
7/8 cup whole wheat pastry flour
3/4 cup buckwheat flour
3/4 cup coarse cornmeal
1 scant cup fine cornmeal
3/4-7/8 cup rice flour

1-1-/3-1-1/2 cups rolled oatmeal
3/4-1 cup rye flour
1 cup rye meal
1 cup corn flour
3/4 cup 1- cup fine whole wheat flour
3/4 cup rolled oats plus 1/4 cup whole wheat flour
7/8 cup whole wheat flour plus 1/8 cup sunflower seed meal

INSTEAD OF AN EGG

1 tablespoon defatted soy or garbanzo flour
3 tablespoons potato flour or tapioca
1/2 cup cooked oatmeal
1 teaspoon Egg Replacer mixed with two table-spoons water (product is a mixture of refined flours and egg whites)

INSTEAD OF OIL

Butter, shortening or oil can be simply omitted in most recipes.

In baking, substitute applesauce or water for the oil used (usually no more than a quarter cup of applesauce per recipe; if more moisture is needed, replace the rest with water).

In cooking, the oils called for usually can be omitted, and an equal amount of vegetable stock or water is used instead.

For pie crusts, cookies and some desserts, cashews or almonds ground with a small amount of water help to hold the ingredients together.

ABOUT SWEETENERS

In general, the amount of sweetening called for in a recipe can easily be cut down. Start by cutting the amount in half. Use malt syrup or rice syrup as sweeteners instead of white or brown sugar. For a different flavor, use unsweetened apple juice concentrate as a sweetner, or ground up dates or raisins.

ABOUT LEAVENING

Use one teaspoon baking yeast dissolved in a quarter cup of warm water to which a half teaspoon of honey has been added. This works well in muffin recipes.

ABOUT NUTS

Nut or seed milk can be used in place of dairy milk in all recipes. It makes a good base for white sauces. Nuts can be ground up and used as a base for spreads or to hold crusts and cookies together. (Proportions: 1/4 cup nut meal to 1 cup water; mix in a blender or food processor).

HERBS, SPICES AND SEASONINGS

As you begin to cook without oils, fats, salt or sugar, you are likely to feel a little lost. These are, after all, the most common seasonings. However, you will soon find yourself more perceptive and appreciative of the unique flavors in foods.

Herbs, spices and other appropriate seasonings can be used to vary and heighten flavor. Use twice the quantity a recipe calls for when substituting a fresh herb for a dry one.

PURCHASING HERBS AND SPICES

Fresh herbs — garlic, dill, basil, oregano, tarragon, parsley, cilantro, mint, ginger and chives — can often be found in the produce section of a grocery or health food store. You can buy potted herbs from a nursery, and grow them at home in a window or your garden.

If you purchase dried herbs and spices in jars, you should read the label to make sure sugar and salt have not been added. If you are thinking of buying them in bulk at a health food store, buy small quantities: herbs and spices lose their flavor with age.

STORING HERBS AND SPICES

Fresh ginger and garlic can be peeled and stored in water or wine in the refrigerator. Fresh herbs can be stored in plastic bags or containers, in the refrigerator or freezer.

Dried herbs and spices should be stored in jars or containers with tight-fitting lids. It is essential that you keep them in a dry, cool place. If you store them near the heat of a stove, they will quickly lose their flavor. Herbs and spices should be discarded when their flavor or aroma becomes weak.

Seasonings that add a licorice flavor:
- fennel
- anise
- star anise
- tarragon

Seasonings that add a salty flavor:
- onion: fresh, flakes or powder
- parsley: fresh or dried
- garlic: fresh, granulated or powder
- lemon: juice or peel
- celery: fresh, seed or powder
- hot spices: cayenne, chili or tabasco

Seasonings that add a sweet flavor:
- vanilla extract
- mint
- cinnamon
- cardamom
- ginger
- mace
- cloves
- allspice
- nutmeg

Seasonings used in ethnic dishes:
- **French:** tarragon, nutmeg
- **Italian:** oregano, basil, fennel, rosemary, garlic, parsley, marjoram
- **Mexican:** chili powder, chili pepper flakes, cumin, cilantro, oregano
- **Chinese:** ginger, star anise, fennel, curry, cayenne, cilantro, hot mustard, garlic
- **German & Scandinavian:** caraway, dill, cinnamon, cardamom, paprika, garlic, lemon
- **Indian:** cumin, curry, coriander, tumeric, fenugreek, garlic, saffron, cinnamon

MENU PLANNING

Quick, what's for dinner? Many people we know would say, "Well, I've got a chicken in the freezer," or "Don't we have some ground sirloin left?" or "Let's broil a couple of steaks!" Those of us who have been raised in the last fifty years are used to planning meals around animal protein. Our "side dishes" are the grains, fruits and vegetables that comprise the main calorie source of meals in much of the rest of the world. To develop healthier eating habits, then, we have to retrain ourselves to eat more like "primitive" man. This means basing our meals around complex carbohydrates, with the occasional meat, fish, or poultry we consume as the side dish!

This transition can be easier than you think! Thinking about the foods of your ethnic background is one way to get your imagination working. Eastern Europeans based their meals around buckwheat, potatoes and wheat. Oriental populations ate large amounts of rice. Africans lived on millet and tubers. South Americans grew yams and plantains. In Mexico and North America, corn, wild rice, squash and beans supplied the bulk of their nourishment. And where would Italy be without pasta?

In this section, we'll give you some pointers on menu planning and a week's menu for weight loss. Also included is brown-bagging advice. Bon Appetit!

EAT FIRST WITH YOUR EYES

Imagine sitting down to a dinner and seeing a white plate with a serving of mashed potatoes, cauliflower and basmati white rice in front of you. Perfectly nutritious, perhaps, but, how boring to the eye! Meals are much more appealing when planned to please all the senses. Season with aromatic herbs that tease the appetite with smell. Contrast colors like deep green broccoli, roasted red peppers, golden ears of corn and rich, purple kidney beans. This meal not only looks beautiful on a plate, but it also packs a powerhouse of good nutrition!

Contrast textures. Try serving crunchy, lightly cooked vegetables with smooth, creamy side dishes. Combine tastes, such as a spicy Indian Dal with a cool, minted vanilla Rice Dream topping, or a fiery Chili with sweet Texas Cornbread.

WHAT TO PACK IN A DELGADO COOL TOTE, LUNCH BOX, OR PICNIC BASKET

Sandwiches on whole wheat, rye or in whole wheat pita pockets with these fillings:

SPREADS/FILLINGS:

- Hummus
- Wheat meat or Nature burgers with barbeque sauce (no sugar)
- Sliced thin: cucumbers, carrots, tomatoes, zucchini, onions red or green bell peppers, with no oil dressing

SALADS:
- Tabouli - Mid-Eastern Wheat Salad
- Potato Salad
- Rice Salad
- Fruit Salad
- 3-bean Salad

(Many of these salads can be stuffed inside a pita pocket)

ENTREES:
- Ratatouille
- Nick's Spicy Brown Rice
- Spaghetti
- Burritos

BREAKFAST FOODS:
- Homemade trail mix
- Banana Bread Pudding Square
- Whole wheat bagel
- Fruit Salad
- Rice custard pudding
- Breakfast burrito
- Fruit juices
- Low-sodium V-8 or tomato juice
- Angeled eggs
- Oatmeal to make in a thermos (just add hot water and wait minutes, stir and serve)

WHEN YOU'RE THE GUEST
- If you can, let the host know in advance your dietary preferences. There is nothing worse than going to dinner and sheepishly

telling your host you cannot eat the food.
- If you discover the food has been smothered with fat or salt, take a bite or two, and then rearrange the food on your plate.
- Eat some of your "legal" food at home before leaving so you are not at the mercy of your hunger and your host's fatty foods.
- Don't be the first guest to arrive. The time before dinner usually means high fat hors d'oeuvres and one too many cocktails! If you do arrive early, request sparkling water with juice.
- Concentrate on low fat appetizers, like raw vegetables, plain crackers or pretzels. Avoid salty and fatty snacks such as anchovies, caviar, cheese balls, sour cream dips, peanuts, etc. If an unwanted hors d'oeuvre is pressed on you, hold it in your cocktail napkin for awhile, then put it down and forget it!
- Circulate and find stimulating conversation. Concentrate on talking and listening instead of eating and drinking.
- Eat plenty of vegetables, a large portion of salad, rolls and other complex carbohydrates. Take only a small portion of the meat dish being served.
- Take fruit for dessert if there is a choice. If not, simply say you are stuffed and could not eat another bite - everything was just

delicious! You can always have some fresh fruit, bread or vegetables from your Delgado Cool Tote in the car or you can eat when you get home if you are still hungry!

WHEN YOU'RE THE HOST

- Prepare the same low fat foods for your guests that you would normally eat. Explain to your guests why you eat the foods you do. Most everyone is enthusiastic about trying the foods even if they do not choose to live with the diet.
- Try gourmet recipes with the recommended substitutions. Dress up the meal for your friends with garnishes. Fix something fancy!
- Potluck dinners work well with a diverse crowd. Everyone can bring their favorites and you will have favorites, too, and can stick with your diet without offending anyone.

One important thing to remember: exposing your guests to your new way of eating may be the most valuable gift you could give them!

AIRLINE TRAVEL:

If business or pleasure finds you traveling on airplanes often, there is no need to worry about breaking your new good food habits. Special meals can be ordered in advance, when you make your reservations. The agent will present a list of different types of dietary plans - fruit plate, diabetic, low cholesterol, vegetarian, and kosher. The best bet is usually a vegetable plate, or low cholesterol meal.

On the low cholesterol meal, you'll still be given fats - margarine instead of butter, so avoid using these. Make sure the vegetarian meal is something comparable to pasta, or a baked potato with vegetables, as opposed to an egg and cheese disaster! This is called an "ova-lacto" vegetarian plate. DON'T ORDER IT! Just ask a few pertinent questions, the same as you would do in a restaurant. But with a little patience, you'll fare well. My fellow passengers usually look on with envy as I enjoy a fresh meal instead of the standard T.V. dinner-type they sit viewing glumly!

The Delgado Cool Tote can be a lifesaver on a long flight. You can nibble on fresh fruit, bread and vegetables hour after hour. You will avoid weighing yourself down by passing up the salty peanuts, candy, buttery sauces and meats.

DELGADO MEDICAL TABLE
OF HEALTHIEST FOODS

EAT DAILY:

1. GREEN VEGETABLES: broccoli, mustard greens, kale, leafy lettuce, etc.
2. YELLOW VEGETABLES: carrots, squash, corn, sweet potatoes, pumpkin, etc.

3. HIGH WATER CONTENT/LOW CALORIE VEGETABLES: tomatoes, cucumbers, celery, cabbage, onions, cauliflower.
4. STARCH VEGETABLES: potatoes, jicama, yams, winter squash, parsnips, etc.
5. FRUIT: pineapple, strawberries, oranges, tangerines, apples, apricots, grapes, watermelon, cantaloupe, cherries, bananas, blueberries, pears, etc.
6. WHOLE GRAINS: brown rice, oatmeal, whole grain pastas, spaghetti, bread, millet, barley, nutty rice, corn or whole-wheat grain tortillas, etc.
7. PEAS: split peas, green peas, yellow peas, black-eyed peas, chick peas, etc.
8. BEANS: pinto, kidney, navy, black, white, lentils, lima, green, mung, etc.
9. CHESTNUTS: (As many as desired)
10. BEVERAGES: Vegetable juice — tomato, carrot, V-8, red bush tea, linden, camomile, Chinese herb; Caffix, Pero, Roastaroma grain drink; fresh water, Perrier water, Poland, low sodium club soda. (Daily as desired).

11. BRAN: Wheat bran — use 1-5 tbsp./day for weight loss and regularity. Psyllium husk, Colon Cleanse or Metamucil — use 2 to 3 tbsp./day, dry to reduce cholesterol.

MODERATE USE FOODS

1. SOYBEANS: Tofu, soybean-meat substitutes — up to 6 oz./day.
2. NUTS/SEEDS: Walnuts, cashews, pecans, almonds, filberts, sunflower seeds, pumpkin seeds, coconuts, brazils, hazelnuts, almond butter, — up to 2 oz./day — 1/4 cup (a small handful of 24 nuts).
3. AVOCADOS: Guacamole — up to 1/4 whole. Black olives — 3/day, Green olives — 6/day.
4. FRUIT JUICE: Dried fruit, juice concentrate, canned, apple butter — up to 8 oz. per day. If triglycerides are over 130 — up to 3 oz./day.
5. LEAN MEATS: Chicken, turkey, fish, cornish hens, flank steak; mollusks (clams, oysters, squid, snail, mussels, scallops) — up to 6 oz./week.
6. DAIRY: Nonfat milk, nonfat yogurt, evaporated skim milk, buttermilk (Alpha Beta or Sacco), lowfat cottage cheese, hoop cheese, Sap Sago cheese, Liteline, Lifetime — fat reduced up to 1 oz./day (due to milk allergies we recommend no more than 8 oz. milk (1 glass nonfat) or 2 oz./ day of yogurt. Instead, we suggest trying lite soy milk or rice milk.)
7. SPICES/CONDIMENTS: Pepper, cayenne pepper, garlic, onion, oregano, "uncatsup" (low sugar, low salt), mustard, chili-salsa, No-Salt Vegit, vinegar.

FOODS TO LIMIT OR AVOID
AND RECOMMENDED REPLACEMENTS

1. CHOLESTEROL

LIMIT: Crustacea (shrimp, lobster, crab, crayfish, etc.) to 1 oz. per week.

AVOID: Egg yolks, organ meats, (brains, liver, kidney, heart)

REPLACEMENT: Egg whites in place of egg yolks, Egg Beaters for occasional use. Replace all foods, (bakery, etc.) that have egg yolks with those that are egg free. Replace organ meats with Vitamin A foods, i.e., carrots, yams or peppers. Use vegetarian based B-12 supplements. Eat iron-rich foods like wheat bran, garbanzo beans, lentils, etc.

2. FAT

LIMIT: Fats to 1 tsp. per day.

AVOID: Vegetable oil-corn, olive, peanut, palm, safflower, polyunsaturated oil, linseed, coconut; margarine, lechithin, shortening; non-dairy creamer, salad dressing, whole milk, lowfat milk, peanut butter.

REPLACEMENT: Use nonstick pans, Pam, chicken broth, no-oil Italian dressing. Butter — replace with butter flavor extract, butter buds, apple butter. Sour cream or mayonnaise — replace with Continental or Weight Watchers nonfat yogurt.

3. CHEESE

LIMIT: 1 oz. per week low-fat cheese
AVOID: Cheddar, Swiss, American, blue Colby, jack, parmesan, mozzarella, ricotta, cream cheese, string, etc.
REPLACEMENT: Liteline, Lifetime or Dorman's.

4. MEAT

AVOID: Sirloin, T-bone, club, hamburger, bacon, sausage, bologna, hot dogs, sardines, ham, duck, pork, lamb, veal.
REPLACEMENT: fruit, juice, concentrate, apple butter, raisins, etc.

5. SUGAR

AVOID: White, brown, turbinated, honey, fructose, artificial (saccharine, sorbitol, aspertame-NutraSweet).
REPLACEMENT: fruit, juice concentrate, apple butter, raisins, etc.

6. WHITE FLOUR

AVOID: White rice, pasta, sourdough, etc. Use only if whole grain is unavailable.
REPLACEMENT: Whole wheat flour products.

7. ALCOHOL

LIMIT: 4 oz. (4 drinks) total per week.

8. CAFFINE

REDUCE: Coffee, tea, soft drinks, decaffeinated drinks.

REPLACEMENT: Roasted grain drinks (Caro, Roastaroma, Pero, etc.).

9. TOBACCO

AVOID: SEE STOP-SMOKING SECTION

10. PROTEIN

AVOID: Powder protein, liquid protein.

REPLACEMENT: Whole food!

11. SALT

AVOID: Salt added to food, soy sauce.

REPLACEMENT: Use other spices on food. Kikkoman salt-reduced soy sauce, up to 1/4 pickle. Use food where salt is listed near end of ingredients.

5

COMPOSITION OF FOODS

There are many books written on how to control cholesterol and lose weight. However, many of these books fail when you get to the recipe section since they invariably contain foods that have cholesterol or fats in amounts that are undesirable. If you want to follow a program that can effectively lower your cholesterol and also can help you to control your weight, then this is the ideal program for you.

There is an easy way to remember whether a food contains cholesterol. If the food once had legs, wings, a tail, could wiggle or move, then it has cholesterol. Obviously chicken and turkey have wings and legs and fish have fins; therefore, they have cholesterol. If you ate a cockroach, it would have cholesterol in it. Don't laugh!! Some people eat fried grasshoppers and they have cholesterol, too!!

If you need to lose weight while you are trying to lower your cholesterol, then simply select the foods that emphasize the soups, a variety of vegetables and fruits, along with oat and corn bran, all of which will help you to lose weight while you lower your cholesterol. If you are trying to gain or maintain your weight, then be sure to select more of the whole grain dishes such as cereal, rice, beans and peas, while eating less of the soup, salad, and fruit dishes.

Select those foods that you enjoy most. Eat them on a frequent and regular basis. By doing so, you will automatically see improvements in your long-term efforts to control cholesterol. Your body will be getting rid of a minimum of 100 mg. of cholesterol a day naturally. And, since you will be eating foods that have no cholesterol in them, you can count on that portion being excreted and not being replaced. Also, by selecting foods lowest in fat and calories, you can expect to reduce your body fat level and reshape your body.

Also, if you eat foods that are high in soluble fiber totaling at least 14 grams or more of soluble fiber per day, you can excrete even more cholesterol than 100 mg. per day. By doing so you will achieve more effective results than if you had resorted to medications for cholesterol control.

The old method of measuring crude fiber used in 1974 was an inaccurate laboratory estimate that has since been replaced by the term "plant fiber," also known as Dietary Fiber. Dietary Fiber is the cell wall components of plant foods not digested in the human small intestines, providing bulk to the stools and almost zero calories.

COMPOSITION OF FOODS

Soluble fiber (gums, pectin and mucilages) commonly found in oat bran, psyllium husk and black-eyed peas help to lower cholesterol and stabilize blood sugar levels when used in amounts equal to 14 grams or more per day.

Insoluble fiber (hemicelluloses or non-cellulosic polysaccharides, cellulose and lignin) commonly found in wheat bran primarily helps to promote regularity and to accelerate weight loss.

The combination of soluble fiber and insoluble fiber equals total fiber. Your intake of "total fiber" should add up to at least 40 to 60 grams per day to promote regularity, proper bowel function and daily elimination.

Vegetables have a high water content and contain the least amount of fat, calories and sodium. This is why vegetables, including potatoes, should be eaten often if you're trying to lose weight. Vegetables also provide a small amount of complex carbohydrates for an efficient source of energy . Vegetables have zero cholesterol, making them safe to eat in unlimited amounts. Fiber is good for weight loss because it has almost no calories. Notice the good source of dietary fiber from onions, artichokes, brussel sprouts and yams. (Fiber remains intact and undigested, leaving valuable bulk to pass through the intestines). Vegetables provide some soluble fiber that helps to draw excess cholesterol out of our bodies.

Beans and peas are low in fat (except soybeans), low in sodium and have no cholesterol.

They are very high in total and soluble fiber (notice black-eyed peas). Beans, split peas, and black-eyed peas are high in concentrated food density, protein and calories. You should limit their use to smaller portions until you reach your ideal weight.

Fruits are the second lowest source of fat and calories. Fruit is the lowest source of sodium and they have no cholesterol. Certain fruits are high in fiber (berries, peaches, prunes). Fruit is good for weight loss and cholesterol and blood pressure reduction.

Cereal, bread and grains are usually low in fat (read labels to be sure there are no added oils or fat), have zero cholesterol and have moderate amounts of sodium and calories. Grains provide an ideal balance of protein for human needs, and they will become the center of your diet after you achieve your ideal weight. Grains are rich in fiber to help prevent digestive disorders.

The highest source of fiber comes from bran. Turn to the section titled "Composition of Foods Chart." Notice that psyllium husk seed (Metamucil) has 8 times more soluble fiber than any other bran. If you add 3 to 6 tbsp. of psyllium a day to your cereal or drinks, you can significantly lower your blood cholesterol level. And if you use fiber in combination with a zero cholesterol diet, you'll get the most effective results. Limit the use of rice bran and wheat germ because they're higher in fat than other brans (3 - 5 grams of fat vs. 2 grams of fat).

Nuts and seeds should be limited to small handfuls in a day, because they're very high in fat with 48 to 84 grams of fat per 4 ounces (cup serving). Nuts are the highest in calories of plant foods. Avocados and black olives are next highest in fat and calories.

Soups with 3 grams of fat or less per 10 oz. can are great for weight loss because they're low in calories and the broth is filling. Some name brand soups are high in sodium (over 1000 mg. per can serving), so make homemade soups whenever you can.

Sugar beverages tend to contribute excess calories and you should avoid them. Fruit juice diluted with mineral water or clean, filtered water are your best choices. Limit liquor to 4 oz. a week or less.

You may be surprised to learn from the food composition list, that poultry and seafood have as much cholesterol as red meat. They are too high in protein (excess protein can cause osteoporosis, fatigue or kidney damage) and they have no fiber. Poultry and seafood are also concentrated in pesticides and toxic chemicals. Reduce or avoid chicken and fish whenever possible.

Salad dressings can be very high in fat, calories and sodium. Notice that some salad dressings are much better than others. Buy no-oil salad dressings.

Desserts are now available low in fat and with no dairy products added (sorbet and Tofutti Lite). Be careful to avoid high fat desserts (pound cake, Haagen Dazs and cheese cake).

Red meat and organ meats contain a concentration of fat, calories and cholesterol. Be alerted that certain cuts of meat are even worse than others. A simple rule of thumb to follow would be to use meats only on limited occasions, and when they are used, only as flavoring and not as the main course. Beef producers are making available leaner cuts of meat. "Lean and Free" are cuts of steak from dairy bulls fed a high fiber, low-fat ration (without growth hormones or antibiotics) and slaughtered before 11 months of age. However, this does not make lean cuts of meat an unlimited use item, because they still have from 35 to 50 mg. of cholesterol per 3 1/2 ounces.

Dairy products, eggs and cheese are extremely high in cholesterol, fat, sodium and calories. They have no fiber and no complex carbohydrates. You need to become aware of the need to avoid these foods.

Fats, oils, margarine and butter are the highest hidden source of fat and calories. Don't be mislead by advertising that promotes "no cholesterol" and ignores the terrible concentration of fat.

Fast foods are high in fat, calories and sodium. Start ordering side dishes like bean burritos or potatoes without cheese. It will make a tremendous difference in the quality of your health.

The section titled "Composition of Foods Chart" needs to be studied carefully so you can make the best food choices while following the Delgado Diet.

6

MAKING THE DELGADO HEALTH PLAN YOUR WAY OF LIFE

All across America there is a new attitude about food. People care again about quality and freshness, and are eagerly exploring new food tastes. They're preparing foods in a new way, using more fresh fruits, vegetables, herbs and spices to create a light, delicious fare. Scorned are the old culinary crutches of the unimaginative cook - greasy fats, salt and sugar.

This section will help you in learning to be a more informed and creative cook. Cooking without fat and salt will open a new world of foods, from old-fashioned regional American foods to international cuisine - plus we will show you how to invent your style of light and healthful cooking.

Begin with a positive attitude! Take pride in your efforts to learn a more healthful lifestyle. There is no need to feel deprived of your old-style foods. Once you begin to use our recipes, you'll know that this is a way of eating you can happily live with for a long and healthy life.

CLEAN OUT THE CUPBOARDS

This is it! Today is the day you're going to begin your new style of cooking. So grab an empty box and rid your cupboards, refrigerator and freezer of those health and vitality-robbing foods. Get rid of foods high in fat, sodium and sugar! Then stock up on the foods listed on our shopping guide!

BE A FOOD DETECTIVE

Government regulations require food manufacturers to list ingredients in order of descending predominance. It would seem to be a simple matter to determine if a food is high in fat, sodium or sugar. But, it is not that easy. Food manufacturers, increasingly aware of consumer concern, have responded not by cutting down unhealthful ingredients, but by making the public THINK that the product is healthier! Various marketing strategies are used to mask the actual levels of some ingredients, especially fat, salt and sugar. Buzz words such as "LITE" are tacked onto a product name, usually with little or no reduction in the fat or caloric content. Sometimes an irrelevant statement is made, such as "NO CHOLESTEROL" boldly printed across a jar, as one nationally advertised peanut butter now proclaims. Of course there is no cholesterol in peanut butter. Cholesterol is only found in foods of animal origin. What they don't tell you is that peanut butter is about 80% pure fat. It's important to learn about label reading to choose foods wisely.

FATS

Studies show that lowering the amount of total fats in the diet has the beneficial effect of reducing the rate of heart disease, cancer, diabetes, stroke and hypertension. An obvious reason to cut down on fats is they are fattening! Fat has twice the amount of calories per gram compared with protein or carbohydrates. Animal foods, especially red meats and dairy foods, can bring the percent of fats in your diet up to 55% of your total daily calories - about the average American diet. Switching to smaller portions of lean animal proteins, such as skinless poultry, fish and nonfat dairy products, is one very effective way to cut down on fat. Another way to reduce fat would be to avoid all meats and dairy products completely. You can do this by focusing on the use of grains, vegetables, beans and fruits as the center of your meals.

Another source of excess fat in the average American diet is fried foods and snacks - potato chips, fried chicken and fish, and french fries. Salad dressings, cooking oils, mayonnaise and nut butters also contribute to a high fat intake. In processed foods, check and avoid foods containing anything but a minimum of these fats:

- Lard
- Beef fat
- Chicken fat, EPA fish liver oil

- Vegetable oils, coconut oil, cottonseed oil, olive oil, lecithin, safflower oil, sunflower oil, canola oil, etc.
- Shortening

Review the fat content of the foods on your current shopping list. Do any of the foods need to be removed or limited? Next, go to your refrigerator and cupboards and note how many of the following fatty, greasy foods you are still eating. Note that any foods containing over 20% of their calories from fat and over four grams of fat per serving should be avoided or limited. You should always eat less than 22 grams and never more than 40 grams of fat per day.

FAT IN FOODS

Food	Percent Calories of Fat	Grams Fat in ½ Cup
Salad oil (corn, olive, etc.)	100	109
Butter	100	91
Margarine	100	90
Mayonnaise	100	87
Bacon	94	70
Cream cheese	91	43
Hamburger (ground beef)	89	16
Avocado	88	19
Peanut butter	85	65
Beef (T-bone steak)	82	20
Egg yolks	80	37
Lamb	76	13
Sunflower seeds	76	34

Cheddar cheese	73	25
Cashews	73	32
Whole eggs	65	14
Mackerel	50	10
Milk, whole	49	5
French fries	43	7
Grains, Beans, Fruits, and Vegetables	1-15	.1-3

HIDDEN SODIUM IN FOODS

Sodium is naturally found in whole foods, such as grains, beans, fruits and vegetables. Unless your physician has advised you to eat a very low-sodium diet, the sodium level of these foods need not concern you. A diet composed of these foods, eaten in their natural state, will supply you with just the right amount of sodium needed for body function. What we are investigating here is the sodium level of processed foods - those jars and bottles, boxes and bags in your cupboard and refrigerator!

You may consider yourself already educated about sodium. You've thrown away the salt shaker and you only buy foods that list salt as the last ingredient. You've made a good start! But it's just not possible to guess the sodium level in a package by reading a simple list of ingredients. The only way to be certain of the sodium content is if the manufacturer has included a nutritional disclosure statement. Guides, such as the Composition of Foods and the Supermarket Field Trip Section of our book, also can tell you the amount in many products. Don't assume that the sodium level is low just because it is listed last. Salt is concentrated, with 2,000 mg. in one teaspoon. In proportion to other ingredients, it may be the smallest volume, yet still be much too high for your health. The United States government recently declared a standard for food manufacturers making nutritional claims. Foods advertised as "low sodium" may have no more than 135 mg. sodium per serving. The manufacturer may claim "No Added Salt," but still use other compounds or ingredients already containing sodium.

OTHER SODIUM COMPOUNDS.

Many other types of sodium compounds are used in food manufacturing. They can contribute significant amounts of unwanted sodium to your diet. They are often "hidden," because they don't necessarily taste salty. A prime example is monosodium glutamate (M.S.G.), commonly used in many processed foods. Some people even use it directly in food preparation. Oriental foods are notorious for its use. You may have used it under the trade name "ACCENT." But what are the other salty compounds?

SODIUM NITRATE - used in preserving and coloring processed meats such as ham, bacon and luncheon meats.

BAKING POWDER AND SODA - found in your pancake mix, biscuits, quick breads and cakes.

BRINE - used to preserve pickles, sauerkraut, corned beef and pastrami, also used in feta cheese.

DISODIUM PHOSPHATE - added to quick cooking cereals such as Instant Oatmeal packages; used as an emulsifier in cheeses, chocolates, beverages and sauces.

SODIUM ALGINATE - used in chocolate milk and ice creams to create smooth textures.

SODIUM BENZOATE - used as a preservative.

SODIUM HYDROXIDE - used to soften and loosen skins of olives, hominy and other fruits and vegetables.

SODIUM PROPIONATE - used to retard mold in bread and cheese foods.

SODIUM SULFITE - used to bleach maraschino cherries.

SODIUM SACCHARIDE - artificial sweetener.

In addition, the following ingredients found on labels are also high in sodium:

SOY SAUCE

TAMARI

AUTOLYZED YEAST

HYDROLYZED YEAST

MISO (different types can have varying amounts of sodium).

WHEN I SEA SALT, I SEE RED

Has anyone ever told you to use "sea salt" instead of regular salt!? This gimmick makes me angry! Advertisements in some health food publications may have led you to believe that sea salt is somehow more healthful than ordinary table salt. While it's true that sea WATER is rich in magnesium, calcium and iodine, sea SALT is so refined that insignificant amounts of these nutrients are left. Sea salt is just as loaded with sodium as any other brand.

You just pay more to poison yourself!

WHAT ABOUT SALT SUBSTITUTES?

A look at the shelf on the "diet" or "health food" aisle of a supermarket will show you several types of salt substitutes on the market. The newest type, the ones we recommend, are creative blends of herbs and spices, with absolutely no salt or sodium chloride added.

Another type of salt substitute is potassium chloride (KCL). It is marketed under the trade names of K Salt Sub, No Salt, Lo Salt and Salt H. Because it is a crystal, like sodium chloride, it has the appearance of salt. Some people find its biting taste similar to salt's effect on the taste buds. Others find it bitter, or chemical, to the taste. We suggest you avoid this salt substitute based around potassium chloride. Also, potassium chloride should not be used by certain people. Although KCL is somewhat safe for people with healthy kidneys, it can cause a dangerous buildup of potassium in the bloodstream of people with impaired kidneys. It also must be avoided by individuals taking diuretics that cause the kidneys to retain potassium.

The third type of salt substitutes are somewhat new on the market. Morton's "Lite" salt and others of its kind are 50/50 blends of potassium chloride and sodium chloride. While it is an improvement over regular table salt, this product still contains 1,000 mg. of sodium in one teaspoon. These are not recommended if you want to control your high blood pressure without drugs.

PROTEIN

You need to limit the use of high protein animal foods if you want to avoid the following problems:

1. **OSTEOPOROSIS** - loss of bone: the greatest single cause of lost bone material in post-menopausal women is the overuse of protein in the diet, especially animal protein, which is more acidic and higher in sulfur than plant protein. Minerals including calcium are pulled out of your bones to neutralize the acid from animal proteins. If you want strong bones and teeth, cut down on the use of high animal protein foods like skim milk, yogurt, cottage cheese, chicken and fish. You can gain

bone density by maintaining your protein intake under 75 grams per day, especially if most of the protein comes from plant foods. By reducing the use of animal protein (meat, cheese, eggs) you can avoid:

2. **FATIGUE, DEHYDRATION, KIDNEY DAMAGE, GOUT & ARTHRITIS** - Foods high in protein leave waste products such as urea, uric acid and ammonia. This buildup of waste acts as a powerful diuretic, which leads to water dehydration of your body tissues and a loss of endurance. Tremendous stress is placed on your kidneys to remove waste, which could lead to failure of one or both kidneys, resulting in death. High uric acid is a well known cause of gout arthritis. To prevent this, keep your total protein intake under 75 grams per day, with no more than 25 grams coming from animal sources. Limit animal proteins to less than one cup per day. For best results, don't use any animal protein (meat or dairy product).

Remember that starch plant foods like grains, fruits and vegetables supply sufficient protein, as you can see from the following chart:

ANIMAL PROTEIN: Limited Use Suggested

FOOD	GRAMS PROTEIN IN 1 CUP	CALORIES OF PROTEIN
Chicken	44	76
Pork	40	45

FOOD	GRAMS PROTEIN IN 1 CUP	CALORIES OF PROTEIN
Beef	30	30
Cottage cheese	30	50
Cottage cheese, lowfat	24	79
Cod fish	27	89
Egg whites	27	85
Skim milk	9	41
Whole milk	9	21

PLANT PROTEIN: Ideal

FOOD	GRAMS PROTEIN IN 1 CUP	CALORIES OF PROTEIN
Pears	1	5
Mushrooms	2	38
Bananas	3	5
Oranges	2	8
Sweet potatoes	4	6
Potatoes	3	11
Rice	5	8
Corn	5	12
Spaghetti	4	14
Kidney beans	14	26
Lentils	16	26
Split peas	16	26

SUGAR

Sugar is present naturally in many foods. There is sugar in fruit and milk, for instance. When sugar is refined from foods, however, it becomes an "empty calorie," with no other nutritional value other than caloric. To metabolize refined sugars, your body must actually draw vitamins and minerals from its storage sites.

Sugar is used as a flavoring and preserving agent in a host of processed foods, from breakfast cereals to ketchup and hot dogs. The highest percentage of sugar in the American diet comes from soft drinks (21), sweets (18), bakery goods (13) and milk products (10). A diet based on fast foods and convenience items is sure to be loaded with sugar, even if you avoid candy and other sweets. Consumers have been concerned about the sugar content of foods for a long time. Some companies in the food industry have responded by lowering the sugar content of their products, or offering non-sweetened versions. It is easy today to buy fruits canned in their juices, for example. Just as often, though, the sugar content of a product is simply disguised. A look at some "health foods" and some types of breakfast cereals will show you a few of the ways sugar is hidden. One way is to use another type of sugar, or to embellish the name, such as "clean raw sugar," or "turbanado" sugar. Some stores will promote products sweetened with honey instead of sugar. Honey is a highly refined sugar, processed courtesy of the bees. It has the same effect on the body as other sugars processed by man. A current marketing gimmick is to combine several types of sugars in one product. A label that might have read, "Sugar, wheat, corn, salt, spices" can appear to be lower in sugar by using, "Wheat, corn syrup, honey, corn, sugar, salt and spices. When reading an ingredient label, be aware of these other names for sugar:

- Raw sugar
- Brown sugar
- Turbanado sugar
- Molasses
- Honey
- Corn syrup, corn syrup solids
- Maple syrup, maple sugar
- Anything ending in -ose, such as fructose, mannose, etc.

Use any type of sugar as little as possible. The best way to sweeten your food is with fresh fruit, applesauce, unsweetened apple butter, small amounts of apple juice concentrate or rice milk. Our Delgado Zero Cholesterol and Weight Loss Cookbook will give you some additional ways to sweeten with a minimum of refined sugars.

FIBER IN THE DIET
WHAT IT IS AND WHY IT'S IMPORTANT

Fiber is the indigestible residue of certain foods, such as whole grains, fruits and vegetables. Meats and dairy foods contain almost no fiber. It is not a single substance, but is composed of cellulose, lignin, hemicellulose, pectin and gums. These five components of fiber all resist the digestive enzymes in your stomach.

WHAT WE KNOW ABOUT IT

Years ago, nutritionists believed that fiber lacked nutritional value. In recent years, however, our thinking has been revised about its benefits. We now know that dietary fiber has a positive effect on several health problems, and more health practitioners are suggesting that we increase our consumption of fiber-rich foods.

Dr. Denis Burkitt, the British physician, began the movement toward high fiber in the treatment of several diseases. He noticed that the Uganda natives he worked with seldom contracted heart disease, colon cancer or diverticular diseases of the bowel. Burkitt concluded their diet was responsible. It was high in vegetable fiber (primarily from whole grains) and low in animal protein, fats, refined grains and sugars. This is directly opposite of the typical English and American diet, with our heavy emphasis on meats, fats, white flour, and sugar foods and drinks. Other studies have shown that high fiber diets may:

- Lower blood cholesterol by reducing the amount of time food is in the digestive tract, thus limiting reabsorption of cholesterol in the bile salts during digestion.
- Improve blood sugar processing in the diabetic, through the gum and pectin components in fiber.

- Prevent constipation.
- Help weight control, by providing a full feeling, increasing chewing time and retarding the rate of ingestion.

CAN YOU GET TOO MUCH FIBER?

Yes, some people get too much fiber from added wheat or oat bran and can have some uncomfortable side effects. An excess can lead to painful intestinal gas, nausea and vomiting. You can prevent this if you maintain a sufficient fluid intake and experiment with the amount of fiber that suits your needs.

If you are eating whole grain breads, vegetables and fresh fruits, you are probably getting the right amount of fiber. You may not need to continue supplementing your diet with added bran after you've achieved your health goals of reduced cholesterol levels, weight loss and regularity.

GRAINS

Grains are high in complex carbohydrates, contain small amounts of fat and moderate amounts of protein, and are cholesterol free.

Whole (i.e., unrefined) grains are high in B vitamins, minerals, and fiber. A whole grain is composed of three parts:

- The germ, high in B vitamins, vitamin E, minerals and essential fatty acids.

- The endosperm, primarily composed of starch, with trace amounts of vitamins and minerals.
- The bran, chiefly indigestible fiber, together with B vitamins and minerals.

During the refining process, the germ and the bran are removed, and only four vitamins and one mineral are replaced. Therefore, whole grains are far more nutritious than their refined counterparts.

Grains are a good source of calories for those who wish to gain weight or maintain weight. If you've been trying to lose fat weight on our program, but your progress has been slower than you had hoped for (as measured by body composition testing), then you may need to reduce the amount of grain servings temporarily, while you increase the vegetables, soups, salads and fruit.

75 CALORIES PER SERVING

1/2 cup barley, cooked	3 tablespoons whole wheat flour
1/3 cup brown rice, cooked	1/2 cup buckwheat, cooked
1 small dinner roll	1 slice bread
3 tablespoons cornmeal	1/2 whole wheat bagel
1 corn tortilla	1/2 cup wheat, cooked
1/2 cup cracked wheat	1/4 cup homemade granola, cooked
1/2 cup rye, cooked	1/2 cup millet, cooked
1/2 cup triticale, cooked	1/2 cup oats, cooked
3/3 cup Shredded Wheat	1/4 cup Grape-Nuts

2 ounces pasta, cooked

1/2 large whole wheat pita bread

COOKING TIMES & PROPORTIONS FOR DINNER GRAINS
GRAINS (1 cup dry measure)

Grains	Water	Time	Yield
Barley (whole)	3 cups	75 min.	3-1/2 cups
Brown rice	2 cups	1 hour	3 cups
Buckwheat (kasha)	2 cups	15 min.	2-1/2 cups
Bulgur wheat	2 cups	15 min.	2-1/2 cups
Cracked wheat	2 cups	25 min.	2-1/3 cups
Millet	3 cups	45 min.	3-1/2 cups
Coarse cornmeal (polenta)	4 cups	25 min.	3 cups
Wild rice	3 cups	2 hours	4 cups
Whole wheat berries	3 cups	2 hours	2-2/3 cups

BEANS AND PEAS

Beans and peas are good sources of protein, carbohydrates, vitamins, minerals and fiber. They are low in fat, and completely cholesterol free. High in calories, they are very helpful for those who are trying to gain weight, or having difficulty maintaining it. If you are trying to lose weight, then you may need to reduce your intake of beans, depending on your progress.

Serving sizes are measured after the beans have been cooked, rather than when dry.

125 CALORIES PER SERVING

1/2 cup azuki beans

1/2 cup black-eyed beans

1/2 cup kidney beans

1/2 cup lima beans

1/2 cup black beans

1/2 cup garbanzo beans

1/2 cup lentils

1/2 cup navy beans

1/2 cup peas, fresh or dried   1/2 cup pinto beans
1/2 cup white beans

COOKING TIMES & PROPORTIONS
FOR BEANS
BEANS (1 cup dry measure)

Beans	Water	Time	Yield
Black beans	4 cups	2-1/2 hrs.	2 cups
Black-eyed peas	3 cups	2 hours	2 cups
Garbanzos (chickpeas)	4 cups	5 hours	2 cups
Kidney beans	3 cups	3 hours	2 cups
Great Northern beans	3-1/2 cups	4 hours	2 cups
Lentils/split peas	3 cups	1 hour	2-1/4 cups
Lima beans	2 cups	1-1/2 hrs.	1-1/4 cups
Baby lima beans	2 cups	1-1/2 hrs.	1-3/4 cups
Pinto beans	3 cups	4 hours	2 cups
Red beans	3 cups	5 hours	2 cups
Small white beans (navy, etc.)	3 cups	3 hours	2 cups
Soybeans	4 cups	4 hours	2 cups
Soy grits	2 cups	15 min.	2 cups

VEGETABLES

Vegetables are composed primarily of complex carbohydrates and water. They are high in vitamins, minerals and fiber. They contain small amounts of fat, moderate amounts of protein and are cholesterol free.

Most vegetables are low in calories and are an ideal food for those who are trying to lose weight.

Vegetables are best fresh or frozen, without added fats, oils, sauces or salt. Canned vegetables are high in salt and should be used only in moderation.

There is no upper limit to the number of servings you may have of the vegetables listed. However, if you want to gain weight, or have difficulty in maintaining it, then you should eat more vegetables from Category C and less from A and B. If you want to lose weight, then select the lower calorie vegies in Categories A and B, while eating less from C.

CATEGORY A: 25 CALORIES PER SERVING

1 cup asparagus	1 cup cucumbers
1 cup bean sprouts	10 cherry tomatoes
1 cup bell pepper	1 cup leeks
1 cup green beans	1 cup cabbage
1 cup bok choy	1 cup zucchini
1 cup mushrooms	1 cup celery
1 cup snow peas	1 cup turnips
1 cup radishes	1 cup cauliflower
1 medium tomato	1 cup squash: summer, crookneck

CATEGORY B: 50 CALORIES PER SERVING

1 cup beets	1 cup carrots
1 cup onions	1 cup broccoli
1 cup eggplant	1 cup rutabagas
1 cup brussels sprouts	

CATEGORY C: 100 CALORIES PER SERVING

1 cup or cob corn	5 oz. white potato
3 oz. sweet potato or yam	1 cup parsnips
1 small white potato	1/2 medium yam
1/2 medium sweet potato	1 cup squash: acorn, butternut, hubbard

FRUIT

Fruits are a good source of vitamins A and C. Yellow fruits, such as apricots and cantaloupes, are high in vitamin A. Citrus fruits, cantaloupes and strawberries are high in vitamin C. Fruits are low in fat, and cholesterol free. They are high in carbohydrates, including sugars and fiber.

Fruit juices and simple sugars are listed here as a sub-category. These are concentrated sources of sugar, with all the fiber removed. Sugars and fruit juices have an adverse effect on health when consumed in large quantities.

Choose several servings (three to eight) per day from the fruit group, with no more than two of them from the simple sugars and juices. Even two servings from simple sugars and juices may be too much for sensitive diabetics, and those with high serum triglyceride levels.

Servings: Three to eight per day, of which not more than two should be from the simple sugars and juices.

50 CALORIES PER SERVING

1 small apple
1/2 banana
3/4 cup papaya
10 large cherries
1 medium peach
1 small tangerine
1/2 cup pineapple
1 small fresh pear
2 dates
2 peach halves, dried

1/4 cantaloupe
1/8 honeydew melon
1 cup watermelon
1 small nectarine
1 small orange
2 medium plums
1 pear half, dried
1 fig, fresh or dried
2 medium prunes
2 tablespoons raisins

3 medium fresh apricots   6 med. apricot halves, dried
1/2 cup berries: blackberries, blueberries, raspberries, strawberries

SIMPLE SUGARS AND JUICES: 50 CALORIES PER SERVING

1/3 cup apple juice   1 ounce juice concentrate
1/2 cup apple sauce   2 teaspoons honey
1/3 cup grape juice   1 tablespoon sugar
1 tablespoon molasses   1/2 cup orange juice
1/2 cup grapefruit juice   1 tablespoon jam or jelly
1/3 cup peach or pear nectar   1/3 cup pineapple juice
1 small glass of wine, 3 ounces
6 ounces beer, light preferred

DAIRY PRODUCTS

Dairy foods vary in their fat and cholesterol content. Nonfat dairy products are the lowest in fat and cholesterol. Lowfat products are the next lowest, with wholefat products highest.

Whenever possible, nonfat products are your first choice, but because of the high protein content, do not exceed two servings per day. Keep in mind that if you are allergic to dairy products, as many people are, then you should avoid using them whenever possible. People who are allergic to dairy products usually find that they can still consume small amounts of yogurt, cottage cheese or Liteline cheese without a bad reaction. This is because yogurt and cheese are fermented, which compared to milk, are a little easier for your body to digest. However, since all the vitamins, minerals and protein your body needs are available in whole complex carbohydrate foods, there is no nutritional need to use dairy products. You should avoid all dairy products to be at the peak of health and feel your best.

Whole eggs and egg yolks are not listed, since they are extremely high in cholesterol. Egg whites are free of fat and cholesterol, and are included in this section.

Lowfat Lifetime cheese, or Liteline cheese can be used in place of high fat, hard, semisoft, and soft regular cheeses. Lowfat cheeses may be used as a substitute for a day's serving of meat, poultry or fish. The maximum serving of any cheese is one ounce per day.

Servings: Up to three times per week.

100 CALORIES PER SERVING

1 cup nonfat milk

1 cup nonfat yogurt

1/2 cup hoop cheese

4 ounces tofu, drained

1/2 cup evaporated skim milk

1/2 cup lowfat cottage cheese

1 cup buttermilk

1 cup lowfat yogurt

6 egg whites

5 tbsp. nonfat powdered milk

MEAT, POULTRY AND FISH

Meat, poultry and fish contain considerable amounts of cholesterol and fat.

Red meat is significantly higher in fat than are chicken and fish. The only red meat cut with a low-fat content is flank steak, which is included here. Shrimp is the only shellfish with an exceptionally high cholesterol content, and has therefore been excluded.

All organ meats - liver, kidney, brain, etc. - are extremely high in cholesterol content, and have also been excluded.

Serving: No more than three times per week (three oz. cooked)

100 CALORIES PER SERVING

albacore	abalone	clams	cod
cornish game hen	crab	flank steak	frog legs
haddock	halibut	lobster	oysters
perch	red snapper	rock fish	salmon
tuna in water	sea bass	swordfish	scallops
chicken, light meat, no skin		turkey light meat, no skin	

7

PROTEIN MYTHS AND FACTS

In this chapter we will look at some myths surrounding protein. The most common myth is that egg proteins are a high quality nutritional source of protein. This has spread through the scientific community as well, and we'll try to help you dispel this myth. Do you still eat two or three eggs per week because you believe that egg proteins are a good source of nutrients? If so, you may develop several degenerative diseases later in life (if you haven't already developed them).

So why has this myth spread throughout our culture? Why do people believe eggs are good for us? Much of the fault lies with invalid rat studies.

In 1914 Osborne and Mendel did their first research studies attempting to determine which foods were the highest quality protein. They decided to use rats as subjects because rats have a short life cycle and are easy to monitor. They found when they gave rats animal-type proteins, such as eggs, meats, cheese, etc., they grew very large. In fact, when rats ate eggs they grew the largest. However, when the rats were fed potatoes, whole wheat, beans, peas or grain as their only food, the rats hardly grew at all.

Scientists thought there must be something nutritionally lacking in wheat, for example, because the essential amino acid, lysine, was too low in concentration to provide for proper growth in rats. (Am. J. Clin. Nutr., 27:1231, 1974). In fact, when they added lysine to the wheat in a diet for rats, the rats grew suddenly. This began the idea of needing complementary proteins or complete proteins. You may have heard of people trying to eat beans and rice at the same meal to be sure they receive adequate protein.

Let's understand what this theory is based on. It is based on the belief eggs are of superior quality, because of the rat studies. But rats are carniverous. They have sharp teeth and claws, and they have a short digestive tract designed to get meat-type protein in and out before it rots. In contrast, humans have a long, convoluting digestive tract designed to handle whole grains, fresh fruits and vegetables. Our teeth are mostly molars for chewing fiber.

Rats grow to full size in 9 weeks time. Humans take nearly 20 years to reach full size. Rats need a concentrated source of protein (rat's breast milk is over 25% protein). In a follow-up study rats were given human breast milk and hardly grew at all because human breast milk is low (under 6%) in protein.

If a nutritionist were to analyze human breast milk based on this information, we would all be led to believe human breast milk is a very poor source of food for infants. Yet, as we all know, it's one of the best sources of food we could supply our infants. When children are growing at their most rapid growth rate, nearly doubling in size, human breast milk allows for maximum growth.

Let's make a comparison to food. Brown rice is merely 6% protein. If you give rice or wheat to rats, they don't grow very well. By comparison, we find children respond very differently. Children given various vegetable proteins, grow just as well, calorie for calorie, compared to animal proteins. (Knapp, Am. J. Clin. Nutri. 26:586, 1971).

One group of children at age 2-5 (a rapid growth rate period), were given only wheat proteins, which is 14% protein. This group was compared with children given egg-type proteins (which is a combination of wheat with lysine to make up for the limiting amino acids). The first group grew just as well, if not better, than the egg protein group. (Reddy, Am. J. Clin. Nutri. 24:1246, 1971).

The claim that animal protein is "superior" to vegetable protein is false. The truth is all natural foods of vegetable origin contain all the amino acids to satisfy human needs. The most recent findings suggest we do not have to combine beans with rice or other vegetables to get a complete protein. Frances Moore Lappe, author of *Diet for a Small Planet,* agrees in her 10th year revised edition human needs are easily met without combining vegetable proteins. In 1988, the American Dietetic Association position paper emphasized it is not necessary to combine protein foods at each meal. The human body makes amino acids that combine in the intestines with amino acids from foods to meet our nutritional needs. Adequate amounts of amino acids and protein will be obtained from a high complex carbohydrate diet supplying a variety of grains, legumes, seeds, vegetables and fruit.

Researcher Dr. C. Lee reported a study (Am.J. Clin. Nutr. 26:702, 1971) in which a group of college-aged students were given two different types of diet, adds support to this contention. One group was given only cheap, starchy white rice, which consisted of just 6% protein. The other group was given chicken and rice. They compared how much nitrogen and protein was absorbed into the body and how much was excreted. Again, everyone was surprised to find the group eating the rice alone had absorbed 20% more nitrogen (or protein) than the group eating the chicken and rice!

There is something special about the vegetable proteins: they seem to have been designed more efficiently for our bodies. We absorb them better than animal-type protein foods. When Dr. Kempner at Duke University gave people protein intakes as low as 22 grams per day (a 94% complex carbohydrate diet from rice and fruit), the result was a protein-sparing effect. The carbohydrates eaten were used for energy, protecting the protein so it could be used for other essential use.

According to Contemporary Nutrition (Volume 5, 1980), a group of men, weighing 154 lbs. each, were given a protein-free diet, and the protein lost from the body was measured. They excreted about 24 grams of protein per day. So we know we need to replace at least 20 to 24 grams a day to meet a person's needs.

It's been established approximately 40 grams of protein would meet anyone's needs. If you make certain you get enough calories and carbohydrates, it will surpass a person's requirements. Eating grains, beans, peas, fruits and vegetables provides over 60 grams of quality protein a day.

According to the National Academy of Science (1980), even a pregnant woman needs only 4 more grams of protein per day than a non-pregnant woman, which would be just 44 grams total. This would satisfy the total known needs of a 9-month fetus.

Another myth is that fish is a brain food. Although the brain does require essential nutrients, it's been found the primary source of food energy to the brain is glucose, which comes from complex carbohydrates. If you do not have enough glucose supplied to the brain, you'd become very hypoglycemic. You might even black out because the brain is in need of the nutrients supplied by glucose. But, it's not really protein that gives us glucose, because protein does not convert nearly so readily into glucose as do the complex carbohydrates.

World-class athletes, including body builders, have recently changed their views on protein. For years they have been telling us they needed large amounts of protein. Chris Dickerson, Mr. Olympia and winner of eleven other pro body-building titles (he's won more body-building titles than Arnold Schwarzenegger), has recently stated, "I used to follow a low-carbohydrate diet, which worked well enough for me to win Mr. U. S. A., Mr. America and two Mr. Universe titles; but since I moved back to California in early 1979 to train for the pro shows, I've followed a low-fat diet since the body prefers to use carbohydrates for its energy needs. I feel more energy in my workouts when I'm on a low-fat diet than when I was on a low-carbohydrate regime."

Carbohydrates are your preferred source of energy. It's the high-carbohydrate, low-fat diet that is the best kind of diet even for a body-builder. Chris doesn't add extra protein foods to his diet. He has found he gets the protein from the whole wheat, beans, peas, fruits and vegetables in his diet.

Mr. Universe, Tom Platz, wrote in "Muscle and Fitness" (Oct. 1984), "If you're going to build an 'out of this world' physique, you need to experiment constantly. Therefore, I increased my consumption of complex carbohydrate foods and immediately noted an upsurge in my strength and size levels. My energy was increased and my blood sugar level seemed to stabilize. Today, I follow a high-carb, medium protein and low-fat diet . . ."

Mr. Olympia 1983, Samir Bannout, uses a high-carb (70%), moderate protein, low-fat (10-20%) diet. So, many top body builders are switching to a Delgado-type plan. Tennis stars like Martina Navrotilova and Jimmy Connors also use a high complex carbohydrate, low-fat, adequate protein diet. The world record in the "Ironman" Triathalon (112-mile bicycle, 26-mile marathon, 2.4 mile swim) was set by Dave Scott, who follows this low-fat approach.

On a strict vegetarian diet (which includes no eggs or dairy products), there would be more than enough protein for muscle growth and maintainence, if an athlete ate enough foods to maintain his weight.

Athletes perspire heavily and lose nitrogen in the sweat. To compensate, a smaller amount of nitrogen is lost in the urine. Only during muscle building are small amounts of extra protein needed. This amounts to merely 25 grams (less than 1 oz.) of protein, which is met by increased intake of food to meet caloric needs of the body.

A gorilla is almost pure vegetarian! They eat tubers, grains, vegetables and fruits and they are one of the most powerful, muscular animals on earth. They don't need to eat meat to be strong.

In elementary nutrition textbooks across the country, there is a great misunderstanding about what our protein needs are. In a textbook by Helen Guthrie, there is a chapter about protein requirements. It has a picture of a big rat and a little rat and the caption reads, "For human requirements." The book states, "Rats will gain more weight on an egg diet than on a whole wheat diet . . ." suggesting there is a correlation between weight gain in rats and tissue protein synthesis. If you read the chapter on protein there are no studies indicating what the protein absorption is when humans eat various foods. The only studies they support that give false credence to the assumption humans need eggs are rat studies! Why do they leave out the human studies?

We found out who sponsors the production of textbooks on nutrition: huge budgets are provided by the Dairy Council and meat industry. They have found it is worthwhile to spend millions of dollars to teach our doctors and dieticians nutrition - based on those old rat studies! Further, they choose to include certain studies they want seen, and leave out those they don't. It's a strong statement to make, but this has contributed to the worst epidemic of degenerative diseases seen in this country's history!

At universities, pamphlets are provided by the

Dairy Council promoting the benefits of eggs, milk and meat proteins. We asked the professors why the Dairy Council is providing so much of this information. They responded by saying the literature is provided free and they can pass it out to their students so our future nutritionists, dieticians and doctors can learn "good nutrition."

What if you still decide you need more protein? Should you buy these protein powders and get as much as you can because you're getting older? We have to disagree strongly with that idea. Our protein requirements are best met by whole natural foods. If you choose to add excess protein to your diet, the result will be devastating, starting with dehydration - a rapid loss of fluids.

Test this for yourself. It won't hurt you to eat a high protein diet for one day. Eat large amounts of chicken, fish, add some protein powders to your meal all day long. See what happens to you - you'll be very thirsty, very quickly. In a couple of hours you'll be surprised at the amount of water you'll need to drink. This happens because your body is building up excess waste products - urea, ammonia and uric acid from the protein that must be diluted by your vital tissue fluid. After several years on a high-protein diet you can develop severe gout, kidney stones, liver disorders and osteoporosis (a loss of minerals, calcium, magnesium and zinc from your bones).

X-rays of bones show us people who eat large amounts of meat, eggs, cheese and protein powders develop holes in their bones as they get older. By comparison, people who eat less protein and more complex carbohydrate foods have greater density and strength in their bones.

Now try another experiment. Two days later switch over to potatoes, fresh fruits, brown rice, whole wheat bread, spaghetti and other carbohydrate foods. Eat these for two days and watch how drastically your requirements for water are reduced! You'll also notice you'll start to feel better.

It is true we need protein for muscles, tissue repair, hormones, antibodies, enzymes and hemoglobin to transport oxygen and clotting ability. Protein is essential to life. Yet we get enough quality protein from whole natural foods that meet our caloric needs, for example:

FOOD	GRAMS OF PROTEIN
1 cup of split peas	16
1 cup navy or kidney beans	15
1/4 cup almonds	6.5
1 cup oatmeal	6
1 whole wheat pita bread	6
1 cup corn	5
2 oranges	2.5

All vegetables contain protein. Don't be misled by people who tell you these foods are a poor quality protein source.

You also may want to include small amounts of low-fat animal products (and B-12 supplements) to your regular diet. You don't need animal protein, but some people enjoy the taste variety. These can be used as a condiment in stews, casseroles, etc. However, an excellent replacement for meat in any recipe would be "wheat meat." Wheat meat is available in some health food stores packaged in a jar, or in the refrigerated section with barbeque sauce called "Wibs." You also could make your own using the recipe in my cookbook under "Vevestake." Try it, you'll like it.

Protein deficiencies (kwashiokor) are due to starvation. A diet of whole, complex carbohydrates contains all the protein you'll ever need, as long as you get sufficient calories. Once you reach your ideal weight, you will need to eat fewer fruits and vegetables and more grains, legumes, peas, nuts and seeds in sufficient quantities to maintain your weight.

The Delgado Health Plan is a proven concept. Within several months you'll feel better than you ever have. This is an opportunity you will benefit from for the rest of your life. Start today.

PROTEIN QUESTION AND ANSWERS
Q. Is it possible to be protein deficient?
A. Protein deficiency generally occurs only due to a lack of calories. It's not the lack of protein in the diet; it's the lack of proper whole foods to meet your needs.

Q. Will I find the best source of quality protein by eating grains, vegetables and fruit?

A. Yes, according to recent studies on humans, your best protein sources are from these foods. Protein is not as efficiently absorbed when it comes from animal sources. This is based on very thorough research with humans instead of rats.

Q. Name some of the best protein sources for humans.

A. The best sources of protein would include whole sprouts, brown rice, grains, whole wheat bread, beans, peas, potatoes, along with a variety of vegetables and fruits. The Delgado Health Plan would give you at least 40 to 70 grams of protein a day, which is more than sufficient. There is no need to include meat, eggs or dairy products for protein needs, unless you're a rat, dog or cat!

Q. Name foods and approaches that would build muscle and gain weight.

A. The best approaches would include the high complex carbohydrate diet with sweet potatoes and whole grains to give you enough calories to build muscle. You would want to begin exercising, especially with weight lifting that will help to build lean tissue.

Q. Is it always necessary to combine vegetables and protein, like rice and beans, at the same meal to obtain a complete protein?

A. No, it's not necessary. The foods supply all the amino acids in each vegetable and grain. Those people who say there are amino acids missing in certain foods are not correct in that assumption. The nutritional analysis of foods shows us the amino acids are present; they're just in different balances and patterns. They don't have to be in the same pattern as eggs, for example. Eggs were not a good comparison base.

Q. Will I have to worry about getting enough protein during weight loss?

A. When you are losing weight you are getting a supply of calories from your body's storage of fat. At the same time, if you eat the high complex carbohydrate vegetables, fruits and smaller amounts of grains, you'll have glucose present to spare your body proteins. Inside the starchy complex carbohydrates there will be sufficient protein to meet your needs. Once you reach your ideal body weight, however, you'll need to maintain a steady calorie intake, possibly adding more grains, beans, yams and pastas to meet your needs.

Q. Are there any people that have special needs to ensure they get enough protein, and how can this be accomplished without adding protein to the diet?

A. Growing children, pregnant women, athletes, and people at or below their ideal body weight will need slightly more protein. This protein need can easily be met by eating less vegetables, soups and fruits, while being sure to eat more whole grain breads, cold cereals, rice, pasta, beans, and yams.

8

EXERCISE
FOR BUSY PEOPLE

Set a goal to exercise twice a day, a minimum of 15 to 30 minutes every morning and again in the evening. If you miss a session, you will at least have gotten in one exercise period a day. Studies show those people who exercise in the morning are more likely to continue exercising one year later, as compared with those who try to exercise in the afternoon or evening.

I always drink two or three glasses of water, and I eat a few grapes, an apple, banana or orange just before I start exercising. You must be well hydrated, otherwise you will become fatigued quickly. In addition, I bring water and some fruit with me to the gym during my workout in case I get thirsty. If you drink fluids before, during and after your exercise, you will find your performance and energy improving dramatically.

Do an exercise that is simple and aerobic in nature. It should employ the largest muscle groups of the body (legs or back). You may want to exercise to an aerobic video tape. You can use a mini trampoline, stationary bike, Nordic track, treadmill or stairstepper. Try out each of these exercises and acquire the necessary equipment to begin your program today.

I have found the motorized treadmill to be

one of the best overall fatburning and conditioning exercises available. You can purchase a good treadmill with variable speed control for under $500. If your home has adequate space, place the treadmill in front of the television or stereo. If you are overweight, you should exercise at a walking speed of between two and four miles per hour. It is important that you can talk during your exercise without becoming completely out of breath. Slow your pace down until you find the most comfortable rate. It has been shown walking one mile will burn nearly as much fat as running one mile.

The key to optimum conditioning is long, slow distances as opposed to short, intense workouts. Exercising at your "target heart rate" according to so-called fitness guidelines may be causing you to exercise beyond or below your capabilities. Certain fitness experts may have led you to believe exercise was of no value unless you worked out hard and intense, at a certain target heart rate (220 - age X 65 to 85%). For most people, a target heart rate of 65-85% will be too intense, and lead to avoidance of your daily sessions. For long term success, a slower, consistent pace will give you the best results. For example, a target of 50-65% for a 40-year-old would equal 90-117 beats per minute sustained during exercise. However, if you can carry on a conversation during your exercise, and go a long, slow distance

(LSD), then you don't have to monitor your pulse rate.

A stairstepper is another great indoor exercise that is a better conditioner than a stationary bike or mini trampoline. You will find you can read a book as you step in place on the footpads. This will help you to lose track of time so that you will exercise for a longer period. However, if you find the stairstepper too hard and intense, and it leaves you "huffing and puffing", then stay with the more gentle bicycle or trampoline exercise session.

A daily walking program of fifteen minutes to one hour a day will burn fat all over your body. If you have a desire to rid yourself of a fat midsection, don't waste time with sit-ups and spot reducing schemes. Lying on a floor and moving your legs is not as effective as moving your whole body upright and supporting your whole weight and walking. Though riding a bike will help those who can't walk due to knee or ankle problems, it's still not as effective as walking. Here again, don't expect one walk to shed 20 lbs. for you. Daily walks, either alone or in addition to other forms of exercise, will have a cumulative effect, and will greatly improve your body's fat-burning capabilities.

Exercise will strengthen your muscles so that your body will burn fat more efficiently. Mitochondria, the power house of the cells, will increase in number, which will improve your body's ability to burn fat. People who are overweight burn fat less efficiently. By following the Delgado Plan of daily exercise and frequent low-fat meals, the process of fat-burning can be accomplished easily.

Daily aerobic exercise will help your body's fat cells to release more fat into the bloodstream sooner to be burned by your muscles. This will allow your body to burn more storage fat during and after exercise, instead of burning mostly glucose. Fit people who exercise daily become "fat burners." Unfit people, who are unaccustomed to daily exercise start out burning mainly glucose and not much fat. Your body has two fuel tanks to choose from, one filled with glucose and one filled with fat (unlike your car that has only one fuel tank of gas.) Eventually, after several months of rhythmic, distance exercise your body will select fat as its preferred fuel. This happens because glucose and storage glycogen is used up so quickly that your body will conserve glucose and become conditioned to burn fat. If you follow our lowfat diet, there will be almost no fat in your bloodstream, so your body will focus on burning released storage fat from your fat cells as you exercise.

9

HOW TO LOOK GREAT BY SHRINKING YOUR FAT CELLS

The Delgado Diet and Exercise Plan is designed so that you can stay on it for a lifetime. Women can develop and maintain that new attractive figure, a leaner body with a firm abdomen, curvaceous hips and a radiant face with the cheeks of a model. Men will have a muscular, firm, better proportioned appearance. You will get compliments from men and women who remember your past struggles with starvation and food restriction diets. Failure, pain, hunger and weakness can all be turned into success, pain free satisfaction and energy on the Delgado Plan.

Women need fat, but in the right places - distributed evenly over the body for a smooth, soft look. For example, a 130 lb., 5'4" ideally proportioned woman, participating in daily exercise classes and capable of running a 26-mile marathon may have 15% body fat. Therefore, 15 to 20% body fat would be a lean, athletic, well-shaped woman. The breakdown of fat distribution may be as follows: 2-4 lbs. for breasts, 4 lbs. of fat in the intestinal area, 4-5 lbs. under the skin and 5 lbs. of fat on the back of each thigh. There is also a need in both men and women for about 15-30 lbs. of essential body fat in the organs and for insulation.

Men look their best when the body fat level is between 5 and 17%. In 1978, when I was overweight, Dr. Bob Girandola of U.S.C. measured my body fat. He used the water emersion method and my body fat level measured over 25%. He told me I was classified as obese! However, after less than 5 months on my lowfat, high carbohydrate diet, and with exercise, my weight had reduced from over 200 lbs. to 159 lbs. Dr. Girandola repeated the test on body fat 4 months after the first test and was amazed that I had reduced to under 9%.

Selecting the right foods for your calorie needs is an effective way to reduce body fat and look years younger. Excess fat leaves a puffy, grotesque look (fatty stomach, hips and face) that makes people look years older.

One study has shown that when subjects were given extra fat added to a low calorie diet, 33% of the fat went right to the fat storage cells. It was discovered by using radioactive tracers placed on the fat in the diet, that the fat was stored instead of being used for fuel. The body is not capable of burning more than a certain amount of fat from the diet. The excess will simply be absorbed and stored by the billions of fat cells of the body. Fat storage cells (adipose tissue) act like billions of small sponges. Excess fat from your diet is absorbed by these fat cells daily, even if you are consuming fewer calories.

Your body receives most of its needed fuel for energy (over 80%) from carbohydrates that break down into glucose. Fat is a secondary fuel that can only be used at a constant slow rate. If you remove carbohydrates from a low calorie diet, your body will continue to burn the same constant rate of fat; however, the rest of your calorie needs will come from glucose stored in your liver and muscles. This stored glucose amounts to less than 12 hours of fuel. After 12 hours of avoiding carbohydrate foods, your entire body storage of glucose will be depleted. When this happens, your body then will quickly begin breaking down your muscle proteins into glucose for fuel, instead of burning more fat. This is why the best diet for you should be very low in fat and high in complex carbohydrates, not just low in calories. Your body can only release more fat from the cells than it stores if there is less fat in your diet and more complex carbohydrates.

Fat provides 9 calories per gram, whereas carbohydrate and protein have only 4 calories per gram. This means fat is twice as fattening as any other nutrient.

We all have different capacities to retain or lose fat. Every day that you eat low-fat foods and exercise fifteen to sixty minutes, you will be establishing a pattern of success. Month after month you will see your results improving as your fat cells shrink. The actual number of fat cells we have is influenced by three critical periods of time during our lives.

The first comes before birth, during the last three months of pregnancy. If your mother was led to believe good nutrition meant eating more eggs, cheese, milk, butter and meat, then the excessive amount of fat and calories would have stimulated an increase in the number of fat cells in the fetus. If your mother had followed a Delgado type of nutritional plan with whole grains, cereals, rices, bread, pastas, beans, peas, fruits and vegetables without added fat, you may have developed fewer fat cells.

The next critical period of fat cell development occurs during the first year of life. If your mother gave you high fat (bottle) formulas and introduced fat and sugar-laden foods, then the fat cells would have increased beyond the expected number. Fat cells could double or triple during the first year after birth. However, if you were breast fed, then your body would have produced fewer fat cells.

In the final, critical period, which is during childhood and youth, the fat cells grow both in size and number. This is followed by another significant increase because of hormonal changes (puberty for teenage girls) and a fatty diet.

However, if you did develop a large number of fat cells, for any of the above reasons, there is no need to be discouraged. The Delgado Program will slim down the size of your fat cells.

It may take several months or even a full year or two to get to your goal of ideal body weight. However, if you consider that this plan will enable you to achieve a fat free body permanently, it's worth the wait, isn't it?

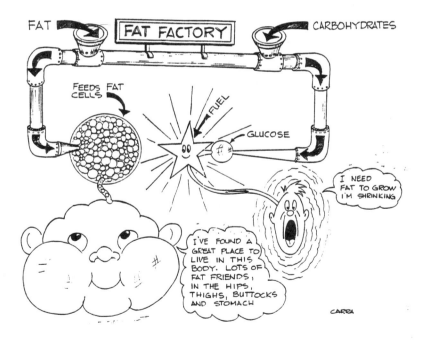

10

FAT LOSS GOALS

Successful participants on The Delgado Plan who lose fat weight permanently, reduce at a consistent rate of 1/4 to 2 lbs. of fat loss per week for women and 1 to 3 lbs. for men. Even very fit athletes with high metabolic rates and muscular bodies that are efficient at burning fat would never burn more than 5 lbs. of fat in a week. In most cases, weight loss more than 3 lbs. a week would be mainly water, body protein and emptying of food from the digestive tract.

If the weight loss is over 3 lbs. per week, you will be losing mostly muscle and water which is deceptive. When you lose muscle, you are losing your best friend in the fight against fat. Muscles burn fat faster than any other body tissue. When you lose muscle, your percentage of body fat may actually be increasing! You could lose as much as 8 lbs. of muscle in a month and up to 12 lbs. of water. Starvation, liquid diets, and portion control (restricting complex carbohydrates) cause you to lose mostly muscle and water, leaving you weak and gaunt-looking. Also, losing body protein (muscle, heart, organs) and water weight is dangerous and can be fatal. Most of the current diet fads promote rapid weight loss to entice you to follow their programs.

Don't be discouraged by slow weight loss - you're losing fat weight on the Delgado Plan. Losing fat weight at a 1 to 3 lb. rate per week is ideal.

The following ideas will help you to understand expected fluctuations in weight: You're body is composed of over 80% water. If you drained and and dehydrated all your body fluids - blood, etc., bone, protein and fat are all that would remain. Fat tissue contains a low percentage of water as compared to muscle that has an extremely high water content.

Your muscles are made up of over 60% water, whereas fat tissue contains less than 10% water. When you lose water on high protein, starvation diets like "Slim Fast" or "Herbal Life" drinks, you are losing a lot of muscle. The emptying of food from the digestive tract, loss of body muscle and water can be done by not eating food for two days, but what have you accomplished? Nothing but a temporary reduction on the weight scale with no change in your appearance and no loss of fat. You need to look at this fact seriously now and consider what is happening. You must reduce your fat intake daily by making the proper food selections or those fat cells in your hips, thighs and stomach will become bigger.

The Delgado Plan increases the complex carbohydrates to over 70% and less than 5% of simple sugar carbohydrates. The average American eats less than 25% complex carbohydrates and as much as 25% simple sugar carbohydrates. Our program also reduces the American diet

from over 43% fat down to under 15%.
The shift in calories will work as follows:

	American Diet	Delgado Plan
Complex carbohydrates	22%	70% or more
Simple carbohydrates	20%	5% or less
Fat	43%	15% or less
Protein	15%	10% to 15%
	100%	100%

This change toward a higher complex carbohydrate food plan will cause some immediate
shift in body water levels accounting for a temporary gain in water weight. However, the great
news is you will notice rapid fat reduction. You'll
look in the mirror and see bulges of fat getting
smaller. Your percentage of fat by body composition testing will show marked drops at the 6
month and 12 month point after starting the
Delgado Plan. It will be easy for you to stay on
the plan for the necessary 12 months or more
to get rid of excess body fat.

However, be prepared for major changes in
body water levels in the first week to three
months. You may even gain weight while you
lose body fat. If you gain weight, don't let it dis-
courage you for these reasons:

1. An increase in carbohydrates allows nearly
60% more glycogen (stored carbohydrate) in
your muscles and liver. Glycogen absorbs
three grams of additional water for each ad-

ditional gram of glycogen. Your muscles will absorb this needed vital water; but this weight gain will be far offset by the amount of fat lost in the next thirty days.

2. Exercise in the first two weeks will cause a significant expansion in blood volume by as much as 30%. This increase in body fluid will make you weigh more on the weight scale, despite appreciable fat loss. Remember, our goal here is fat loss to get rid of those unsightly bulges, not just a deceptive and temporary water loss.

3. High fiber complex carbohydrate foods provide needed bulk to the stools. Your intestinal tract holds up to 10 lbs. worth of food which can add to your weight. This satisfied, full feeling may be a new experience for you if you're accustomed to starvation liquid diets or limited portion control plans that always leave you feeling empty. Stepping on the weight scale in the first month may be discouraging; but, 12 months after starting the program you will appreciate how sensible and easy it is to eat high fiber, low-fat foods.

4. Menstrual cycles can cause several pounds of fluid retention. This is one reason women should only weigh themselves from month to month and not be worried about weekly changes in weight.

5. The Delgado Plan can help you reduce your dependency on medications such as diuretics or Beta Blockers that will cause a significant regaining of vital body water. This is another temporary change that your body will adjust to in a matter of weeks. (Be sure to have your dosages of medications monitored by a physician willing to help you reduce your dependency on chemicals.

11

PESTICIDES EXPOSURE HIGHEST IN MEAT FISH, DAIRY

If you want to lose weight you must eat a large amount of fruits, vegetables, salads and vegetable soups; smaller amounts of grains and beans; and little or no meat and dairy products. The concern of pesticides is not overlooked here in regard to eating more fruits and vegies; but, let us remind you that eating closer to the origin of the food chain - fruits, vegetables, grains, beans and peas - is much safer than eating high on the chain (animal products) because of biomagnification.

Biomagnification is the increased concentration of chemicals, pesticides and toxins that results when animals eat grains and vegetables exposed to pesticides, which concentrate 1000 times in the animal's fat. When you eat the animal, the pesticides and heavy metals like mercury or lead can concentrate in your body not just double, but 1000 X 1000 or one million times! The concentration of these potentially deadly chemicals increases the higher you eat on the food chain. Meat, fish and dairy products expose you to the highest concentration of these deadly chemicals. Grains, fruits, and vegetables are comparatively safe.

Small fish and plankton consumed by larger

fish like tuna or swordfish, and eventually eaten by humans, have potentially high concentrations of chemicals that are dose related. The higher the dosage, the more dangerous the chemicals become as they concentrate in your body to lethal levels that may induce cancer or liver failure. Meat, chicken and fish have 10 times more pesticides than plant foods: fruits, vegetables or grains.

Drinking the milk of animals (cow or goat) is equally dangerous because of the buildup of harmful substances that end up in the secretions (milk) of the animal. Dairy products (milk, cheese, sour cream and eggs) have 5-1/2 times more toxic pesticides than do plant foods. A woman who eats low or at the origin of the food chain (fruits, vegetables and grains) will be eating lower-fat foods with fewer chemicals, and in turn with fewer chemicals for her baby. According to the New England Journal of Medicine, March 26, 1981, only 2% of mothers' milk from women eating only grains, beans, fruits and vegetables (no meat) was found to contain significant levels of DDT and other toxic chemicals. By contrast, 100% of mothers eating meat and dairy products produced breast milk with significant levels of DDT, pesticides and toxic chemicals.

Health-conscious people prefer to buy organic fruits and vegetables. Purchasing organic, seedless red and green grapes, potatoes, apples or carrots is worth the extra 10 to 60 cents a pound to avoid chemicals and pesticides. The average person eats at least 4 lbs. of food a day, so for a mere $1.40 extra a day we will be supporting those farmers who care about the future generations. This may force other farmers to begin farming pesticide free.

If you do buy non-organic fruits and vegetables, like cabbage or lettuce, then take a moment to peel the outer leaves. Rinse broccoli, cauliflower, nectarines, pears or grapes in water. You may want to soak them briefly with a dash of liquid soap or use one of the vegetable cleaner solutions currently available at health food stores. Peeling non-organic apples may be necessary, since the wax seals the pesticides onto the apples. It's far better to eat the fruits, vegetables and breads as they are, as compared to the fast foods and deadlier T.V. dinners. Less than 7% of the pesticides we consume comes from grains, fruits and vegetables. However, 55% of the pesticides comes from meats and 33% comes from dairy products.

12

AVOID THE MISTAKES OF OTHER PROGRAMS USE THE DELGADO SIX

To lose weight, stay fit and have energy, you need to stop adding fat to your diet now, today! The four food groups are this country's worst diet mistake - it forces you to select food from fattening categories such as meat (beef, pork, chicken, fish) and dairy products (cheese, milk, yogurt, butter, etc.). Two of the four food groups are extremely concentrated in fat. That is partly why the American diet gets nearly 50% of its calories from fat. Grains, vegetables and fruits are the only acceptable foods from the basic four. Diets by Weight Watchers, NutriSystem, Jenny Craig, Diet Centers and the like are forcing you to follow the old four food groups. You are led to believe that you cannot have a "balanced diet" without keeping meat and dairy products in your diet.

The four food groups got started many years ago to simplify the public need for food during war time. The basic four groups have led many people to consume products to which they are allergic, like milk and other dairy products. Also, people with an excessive capacity to retain fat are struggling to overcome the inherent disadvantages of consuming meats and dairy products. Meats and dairy products are totally without fiber, deficient in complex carbohydrates and low in water content. Chicken, fish, red meat, yogurt, cheese, milk and butter are generally higher in sodium, fat, calories and cholesterol than complex carbohydrates: starches, fruits, vegetables, beans and peas. Cheese, milk, eggs, meat and oils are concentrated in food density. Put simply, every bite of food from meat or dairy products is so concentrated in calories that it goes right to your fat storage. This concentrated source of calories can't possibly be used by sedentary people.

You are being misled by sales and marketing gimmicks that trick you into buying high fat, high sugar and salty products with taste-tempting pictures and healthful sounding names like Weight Watchers. The name Weight Watchers automatically means low-fat, light foods to most people, which is not always true when you look at the labels of their frozen foods. The only redeeming value of these weight control programs is you are asked to eat fresh fruits, vegetables and whole grains besides the frozen foods. It's these fresh, whole natural foods that keeps the dieters intake of fat and cholesterol in check in spite of the fat and cholesterol-laden packaged foods.

Weight Watchers		**Swanson's**
So. Fried Chicken Patty	VS	Fried Chicken (white portions)
FAT:	16 grams	16 grams
% of fat:	53%	41%
Serving Size:	6.5 ounces	6.5 ounces

So called diet foods like Weight Watchers and Lean Cuisine are as high or sometimes higher in fat by percentage of calories than the regular food brands. The average frozen food line of Weight Watchers contains 37% fat (11 grams of fat, 290 calories, 60 mg. of cholesterol and 800 mg. of sodium.) Lean Cuisine averages 9 grams of fat, 260 calories, 60 mg. of cholesterol, and 930 mg. of sodium. The reason they may have fewer calories is that they give small portions or they use non-nutrient fillers and thickeners. The unsuspecting, uninformed public blindly trusts the name Weight Watchers, NutriSystems and Jenny Craig.

For example, here is the entire ingredient list from the Salisbury Steak Champignon, Jenny Craig's best selling prepared "diet" frozen dinner: Cooked **beef,** water, cooked potatoes, carrots, green beans, onions, **cheddar cheese,** bread crumbs, **eggs,** mushrooms, **white wine, margarine, vegetable oil,** demi glace (wheat flour, starch, **lactose,** dehydrated onions, **salt,** tomato starch, hydrolyzed plant protein, **vegetable oil,** yeast extract, **beef extract, sugar,** caramel, corn starch, **wine powder,** spices), modified food starch, tomato paste, **nonfat dry milk, salt,** flour, natural flavorings, **beef flavor (salt, corn syrup solids, beef fat,** hydrolyzed plant protein, celery, and other spices, onion powder, starch, **beef extract,** caramel color, garlic powder, spice extractives of pepper, **di-**

sodium inosinate, **disodium** guanylate), Worcestershire sauce, spices, **chicken flavor (corn syrup solids, salt, chicken fat, all vegetable shortening [soybean, cottonseed oil],** onion powder, starch, **disodium** inosinate, **disodium** guanylate, spice extractives of celery and tumeric), garlic, parsley, xantham gum, annato color, **artificial color** (contains FD & C Yellow #5.)

Now that you've read this list of ingredients from their label, does this look like a food that would be good for your health? Your cholesterol level? Or for weight loss? It's no wonder why you have to eat such small portions of these frozen "diet" dinners. We challenge you to read the labels of other "diet" system programs. They derive most of their profit from selling packaged foods.

The name on a label can say anything because it's considered part of the title. So beware of misleading words on food products like "pure virgin" olive oil, "natural" sugar and "unrefined" flour. Remember to look on the back or the bottom of the container and read the nutrition information under "ingredients." The ingredient list is strictly controlled by the Food and Drug Administration (FDA). The listing must be accurate, be in a particular sequence and leave nothing out. Always look for oils, butter, margarine, sugar, fructose and salt and if any of these fattening ingredients are listed first on the label, you know the food is concentrated in calories.

As you read labels, also look at the total grams of fat and if there are more than four grams of fat per serving don't buy it. If the food product has less than 4 grams of fat, then it's generally okay to buy. This simple rule of buying food products with zero, one, two or three grams of fat per serving will help to keep your average fat intake per day to less than 20 grams of fat and under 20% of total calories from fat.

The average American man or woman consumes over 125 grams of fat per day adding up to a whopping 43% fat diet. Multiply the number of grams of fat by 9 and then divide that number by the total calories listed on the label to determine the percentage of fat. For example, Promise margarine, approved by the American Heart Association has 10 grams of fat and 90 calories per tablespoon (10 grams X 9 calories/gram = 90/90 = 100% fat!). Promise margarine, Heart Smart and "I Can't Believe it's not Butter" have the most amount of fat of any foods on Earth! Read the labels. The first time you go to a market armed with this information you will be shocked at the amount of fat in slickly packaged foods. 2% low-fat milk has 32% fat with it's five grams of fat per 140 calories in 1 cup. It should be called high-fat milk, and whole milk with its 50% fat and 9 grams of fat should be called greasy milk. Figurines, the diet bar, has 5 grams of fat per serving, exceeding 45% fat. This should be called a "fat" bar, not a diet bar.

Now, let's review the latest liquid drink craze - "Slim Fast." The following is a comparison of a 1200 calorie-per-day intake:

THE DELGADO PLAN (one day example)	VS	LIQUID SLIMFAST DIET
4 pieces of fruit (banana, peach, pear, nectarine		3 liquid Slimfast 3 oz. water packed tuna
1 large potato, w/salsa		1 tsp. diet mayonnaise
2 slices of bread, w/apple butter		lettuce, tomato bread, 1 slice
2 bowls of soup		1 diet coke
2 large salads, w/oil-free dressing		
1 cup of brown rice, or pasta		
1 bowl of sorbet ice cream		
High fiber, low fat, no cholesterol		High protein, sugar and cholesterol

The Slim-Fast directions recommend you use their product three times a day for breakfast, lunch and as a snack, which adds up to as much as 600 calories. For dinner eat a specified meal, such as the one above. The ingredients of the Slim-Fast are whey powder, sucrose, nonfat dry milk, dextrose, calcium caseinate, purified cellulose, soy protein, bran fiber, fructose, natural and artificial flavors, malto-dextrins, carrageenan, lecithin, DL Methionine, aspartame, vitamins and minerals. This product contains four forms of sugars. It is also concentrated in dairy product from whey, nonfat milk and calcium caseinate.

Another gimmick product is Ultra Slim-Fast with the following ingredients: sucrose, nonfat dry milk, whey powder, corn bran, calcium caseinate, soy protein isolate, purified cellulose, cellulose gum, <u>fructose</u>, guar gum, malto- dextrins, carrageenan, <u>hydrogenated soybean oil</u>, <u>artificial flavors</u>, lecithin, DL <u>Methionine</u>, <u>aspartame</u> with phenylalanine, vitamins and minerals.

The only difference between the two forms of Slim-Fast is a small amount of added fiber. They also contain several harmful ingredients that may elevate triglycerides and cause allergic reactions. These products are only for quick weight loss, but do not help to change your bad eating habits.

In 1990, 20 million Americans spent over one billion dollars on liquid weight loss products and liquid fasting programs. Well known celebrities advertise and endorse these fads, but they rarely keep the weight off. You may have heard of Oprah Winfrey's recent weight gain. As you recall, two years ago she lost 67 lbs. thanks to a 400-calorie-a-day liquid protein plan. At that time, she vowed to never be fat again. Unfortunately, she has now regained all of the weight she lost initially, plus a few pounds more! The problem with these fad diets is that they do not retrain your eating habits. After you lose weight on these plans, inevitably you will gain it back.

Why not introduce these dieters to the Delgado Health Plan to get the best weight loss, save money, and improve total health? You will be successful in losing weight if you follow the Delgado

 Plan, which encourages you to change your eating habits for a lifetime.

Become knowledgeable and don't be afraid to eat more of the whole natural foods on the Delgado Plan. Your friends might lose weight faster initially on their Weight Watcher's or starvation liquid diets, but you will pass them up in a few months and never be fat again, unlike your friends who will always struggle until they also learn the Delgado Plan.

You will lose fat weight effectively if you eat less than 20 grams of fat per day and never more than 40 grams. Your total percentage of calories from fat should be under 20%. This is the Delgado 20-20 rule: less than 20 grams of fat, under 20% fat to lose fat and keep it off. Your calorie intake will be under 2000, with an average of between 1000 and 1700 calories per day. To keep under 1700 calories per day just be sure to eat generous helpings of soups, fruits, vegetables, potatoes and complex carbohydrates without added fats and sugars. Eat more of the fiber and balanced foods that nature has provided.

Here are the DELGADO SIX FOOD GROUPS:
1. Green vegetables
2. Yellow/orange vegetables
3. Tuber-root vegetables (potatoes, beets, etc.)

4. Citrus and non-citrus fruits
5. Grains (two or more types per day) plus a Vitamin *B12 fortified cereal
6. Beans and peas (green, Chinese, split, black-eyed, chick)

*or B-12 supplements preferably in combination with a B-complex.

Note: include a weekly serving of sea vegetables (kelp, kombu, wakame, nori) and nuts and seeds for additional trace minerals.

Low-fat meats, chicken, fish, turkey, flank steak and nonfat dairy products should only be used as a condiment and never as a main dish (you may choose not to use any meat or dairy product). You should say, "We're having potato pasta casserole," instead of saying, "We're having chicken tonight with a side dish of vegetables."

A 1989 survey by the California Department of Health of 1000 consumers discovered that over 25% of those questioned ate no fruits or vegetables on any given day. Nearly two-thirds of Californians don't eat enough fruits and vegetables. Mass media advertising has led to reliance on fast food burgers, frozen dinners and fatty dairy products. The information in this book will show you how to improve your diet dramatically and gain control over hunger and improper food selections.

13

HOW TO INCREASE YOUR ENERGY

One of the key reasons people participate in the Delgado Health Plan is to increase their energy levels. The complex carbohydrates are your best source of energy. Fat provides you with less quality energy. Protein would be the least acceptable energy source and cause the most fatigue. To have more energy, therefore, eat potatoes, vegetables, fruit and whole grains that are high in complex carbohydrates.

Plan ahead, carry food with you in a sack lunch, ice chest or a Delgado Cool Tote as I carry with me. This will maintain even glucose levels, giving you a high energy level. The moment you begin to feel weak, an empty stomach or hungry, go ahead and eat lightly. Frequent small meals of complex carbohydrates will be digested into glucose at a slow, consistent rate. Big, heavy meals tend to lead to a build-up of fat in the blood know as triglycerides.

Triglycerides are the way fats are carried in the blood and are stored in your fat cells. Pinch the fat on your body and you are pinching triglycerides. To experience high energy, you must maintain low fat levels in your blood. Strive to keep your triglyceride levels under 100 mg. and total lipids ideally under 500 at all times during the day, especially after eating.

Fasting for blood tests have misled people and physicians into ignoring poor dietary habits. By eating frequent, small meals that are low in fat, you can maintain low fat levels in your blood all day and night. This will allow for excellent circulation. The red blood cells will flow freely to carry the maximum amount of oxygen to your brain and all the cells of your body. One fatty meal can cause the blood to become sticky, resulting in clumping of the red blood cells for over 9 hours. If less oxygen reaches the brain, you will become sleepy and tired. This is probably why so many people drink coffee (caffeine is a drug stimulant) to try to stay awake and alert. However, by maintaining lowfat triglycerides and total lipids you will experience an incredible increase in energy as more oxygen reaches your brain.

The following steps are necessary to reduce fat in your blood:

1. Avoid all oils: polyunsaturates like corn oil, safflower oil, etc., monounsaturates like canola oil, olive oil, etc., and saturated fats found in butter, cheese, red meat, etc.

2. Avoid excessive use of sugar, alcohol, fruit juice or dried fruit. Sugars convert into fats if used beyond your caloric needs. Sugars are devoid of fiber so they rush into your bloodstream too quickly and turn into fats.

3. Maintain your ideal weight - obesity can cause high fat levels in the blood. In order

to have more energy, you must achieve your ideal body weight. If you are currently overweight, choosing all the recommended foods and exercising daily, you may not begin to experience high energy levels until you reach your ideal body weight. If you are carrying 10 to 40 extra pounds on your body and that extra weight is in the form of fat that can enter your bloodstream at any time and slow you down, just as if you had eaten fat. You can reach your ideal body weight by following the recommendations we offer in this book.

4. Exercise daily to maintain good circulation and low fat levels. Daily exercise will begin to fire up your system to give you more energy. If you do the minimum of 15 minutes a day, that is fine. But why not plan to do 15 minutes in the morning and 15 minutes more at night? By exercising in the morning, you will burn fats that have accumulated during the night while you were sleeping and inactive. Since your triglycerides will be lower, you will have more energy throughout the day. Then at the end of the day, when there is a tendency to have a slight elevation of triglycerides, exercising again for 15 minutes will reduce the fatty levels in your bloodstream.

If you want to maintain high energy levels all day long, avoid excessive or intensive exercise. Long, slow distance exercises (walking,swimming, light weights) are better than fast, overly demanding runs and heavy weight training sessions. If you are an athlete or you are accustomed to intense workouts, anticipate a need for several additional hours of sleep to allow your body to recover each day. Training to the point of muscular failure on every exercise is terribly taxing to your energy levels. Start your exercise plan slow, be consistent and you will look forward to each day with excitement and vigor. If you find yourself avoiding exercise sessions, you probably have been training too hard.

5. Reduce stress by focusing on the good things in people and in life. If adrenaline builds up, it can increase blood fats for several hours.

Have your triglycerides, cholesterol and total lipids checked every three weeks until you can maintain ideal levels on a regular basis. After consecutive low readings, you can check your levels every three months to be sure you're still on the right track.

Make sure you get enough sleep each night. Most of our participants notice they require much less sleep as they eat better and exercise. You should feel rested and good in the morning without needing coffee, tea or cokes all day. A thirty minute nap during the day may be beneficial for people who work long hours (12 to 16 hours a day.)

Your physiology, posture, stance and walk are also important to feel energetic. If you slump and slouch you will feel tired. Try sitting up straight and erect and you will notice an immediate improvement.

Some people suffer from "chronic fatigue syndrome", which can be caused by a number of different conditions. See a doctor to check your thyroid, blood counts, B-12 and iron for anemia, possible viral conditions like Epstein-Barr, mono, etc., allergies and other metabolic diseases like cancer. The Delgado Plan can serve as a cornerstone to enhance treatment and in many cases provide full recovery from various energy robbing diseases.

The final key to high energy is to fill your mind with good news, good thoughts, read positive books, listen to motivational tapes, attend church sermons and success seminars.

14

FOOD SELECTION
AND LABEL READING

Did you ever notice how easy it is to buy unplanned items at the supermarket? Snacks at the checkout counter, "specials" on the aisle-end gondolas and manager's super savers at the meat counters all seem to jump into your shopping cart. Supermarket marketing and merchandising is a very sophisticated, multibillion dollar industry. It's all too easy to be manipulated by packaging and advertising. Here are some pointers to make you supermarket smart:

- NEVER go shopping when you're hungry. People who shop on an empty stomach buy 10 to 20% more groceries than when they are full. This advice can save both your health and your bank balance!

- Think of the shopping cart as your stomach. What goes in the cart goes inside you. It's easier to resist temptation in the store than when the food is in your kitchen.

- Don't buy "bad" foods for the kids or guests. You know who will want just one bite! Make the treats you serve others real treats - wonderful fresh fruits or dishes you've made yourself.

- Generally, the foods on the perimeter of the store are the fresh foods - the produce fruits and vegetables. The less you wheel your cart down aisles of cans and boxes, the better.

- Plan your shopping after you've planned your menu. And plan your menus around complex carbohydrates - grains, beans, fruits and vegetables, not animal proteins.

SUBSTITUTION LIST

The following list will help you in preparing your shopping list to substitute for the items you discarded today.

GOODBYE TO:	BETTER BUY:
Table salt, Accent, Season Salt, M.S.G.	Lemon, Pepper, Spike, Mrs. Dash, Instead of Salt
Garlic salt	Garlic powder
Onion salt	Onion powder
Soy sauce, tamari	Low-sodium soy sauce (use in very limited amounts), 500 mg. in 1 tablespoon
Bouillon cubes	No salt added vegetable
Worcestershire sauce, A-1 steak sauce	Mrs. Dash, no salt added steak sauce
Canned soup	Low sodium, lowfat, or homemade soups
Artichokes marinated in oil/salt	Artichokes canned in water low salt
Canned vegetables in salt	Fresh, frozen or canned, salt-free
High oil/salt salad dressings	No oil/salt-free salad or homemade
Non-dairy creamer	Lite soy milk, rice milk
Sugar	Fruit concentrates
Bacon, sausage, ham, luncheon meats	Wheat meat with spices

Pickles, relish	Salt-free pickles
Mustard, catsup	Salt-free mustard, catsup
Most cheeses	Non-fat cheeses
Whole milk, cream	Lite soy milk, rice milk
Cereals with salt	Nutri-Grain, Shred-
or sugar added	ded Wheat, Nutti Rice, etc.
Ice cream w/sugar	Nuevelle Sorbet, (at health
	food stores)
Jello, puddings	Add your own sweetener gel-
	atin desserts
Jam, jelly, preserves	Low sugar or sugar-
high in sugar	free fruit preserves
Soft drinks	Sparkling mineral water (ex-
	cept Vichy)

FOOD LABELS
HOW TO CALCULATE THE TOTAL
% OF FAT, PROTEIN AND
CARBOHYDRATE

The calculations presented below can be used to determine what percent of a store-bought food product is fat, what percent is protein, and what percent is carbohydrate, so you can decide if the food is on the Delgado Diet or not. A general guideline is to limit anything greater than 18% protein and anything greater than 20% fat. Complex carbohydrates (but not sugars) are free!!

The data you need to memorize to do these calculations is:

- 1 gram of protein is approximately 4 calories.
- 1 gram of carbohydrate is approximately 4 calories.
- 1 gram of fat is approximately 9 calories.

Now you can tackle any label providing nutritional information. Here is how:

EXAMPLE 1.
NATURAL WHOLE GRAIN BREAD

Data given on the label:

140 calories per serving

6 grams protein per serving

25 grams carbohydrate per serving

2 grams fat per serving

A. PROTEIN:

6 g. protein X 4 calories / g. protein = 24 calories divided by 140 calories X 100% = 17% protein

B. CARBOHYDRATE:

25 g. carbohydrate X 4 calories / g. carbohydrate = 100 calories divided by 140 calories X 100% = 71%

C. FAT

2 g. fat X 9 calories / g. fat = 18 calories divided by 140 calories X 100% = 13% fat

CONCLUSION: This whole grain bread would be okay to include in your diet because the total % of protein and fat are less than the Delgado Diet maximums listed.

EXAMPLE 2.
OATS, N'HONEY BREAD

Data given on the label: 150 calories per serving 6 grams protein per serving 23 grams carbohydrate per serving 4 grams fat per serving

A. PROTEIN:

6 g. protein X 4 calories / g. protein = 24 calories divided by 150 calories X 100% = 16% protein

B. CARBOHYDRATE:

23 g. carbohydrate X 4 calories / g. carbohydrate = 92 calories divided by 150 calories X 100% = 61% carbohydrate

C. FAT:

4 g. fat X 9 calories / g. fat = 36 calories divided by 150 calories X 100% = 24% fat

CONCLUSION: This bread would be marginally unacceptable because the % of fat is above the maximum.

EXAMPLE 3.
CHEDDAR CHEESE

Data from Nutrition Almanac or on some labels:
114 calories per serving

7 grams protein per serving.

.4 grams carbohydrate per serving

9.5 grams fat per serving

A. PROTEIN:

7 g. protein X 4 calories / g. protein = 28 calories divided by 114 calories X 100% = 26% protein

B. CARBOHYDRATE:

.4 gram carbohydrate X 4 calories / g. carbohydrate = 3.6 calories divided by 114 calories X 100% = 3% carbohydrate

C. FAT:

9.5 g. fat X 9 calories / g. fat = 86 calories divided by 114 calories X 100% = 75% fat

CONCLUSION: This cheddar cheese is 75% fat and only 1 oz; has over 9.5 grams of fat. That means if you added this to a "20% calories from fat diet," you would push the total fat intake for the day to over 25% fat! Notice also this cheese has 26% protein, and that any food over 15% protein is excessive and can promote osteoporosis and fatigue. The carbohydrate content is only 3.6%, and this is far below the recommended 60% of calories from carbohydrate.

NOTE: Sugar should be considered a simple carbohydrate (not complex). The closer it is found to the beginning of the ingredient list the greater the % of sugar present. Though some labels are starting to list the amounts of simple vs. complex carbohydrates present, this is not always done and you will often have to make an educated guess about the total % of sugar present (more than 10% sugar is considered excessive.

POINTS TO REMEMBER IN LABEL READING

This section will help a health conscious individual, such as yourself, to be informed about reading food labels at the supermarket. The intelligent food shopper can scrutinize labels and detect hidden fats, sugars, sodium and cholesterol.

- Ingredients are listed in order of descending predominance.
- If a product claims to be "low sodium," they must include the sodium content. Be sure to note the serving size.
- To determine the percent of fat in a product, multiply the grams of fat by 9, then divide by the total calories. Look for items under 20% fat.
- Review the code names for fat, salt and sugar. Avoid foods with added sodium compounds, and high percentages of fat and sugar.

The food manufacturers decide the serving size for their product and give nutritional information on a "per serving" basis. Smaller serving sizes are sometimes used to try to make their foods appear to have less fat, sodium, etc.

Different sugars may be listed as different ingredients, very often making it difficult for most people to tell just how much sugar would be in that food. For example, in one food item, sugars could be listed as corn syrup, dextrose and brown sugar.

To make matters worse, a label is currently only required when a manufacturer makes a claim about the nutrient content of a food. This means about half of all foods have no nutrition labeling. For example, labeling is only required if the food has a written claim like "low calorie" or "low sodium," or when the food has been fortified with vitamins and minerals. When referring to sodium or calories, the FDA has only defined a few claims ("low" and "reduced"). If the claim is being made about fiber or fat, ambiguous terms generally are used such as "lite" or "natural." These terms allow the food manufacturers to say whatever they wish, without being forced to reveal an itemized label.

On your next trip to the market, you can make better decisions on which food products to purchase, because your decisions will be based on the quality of the food and not just on the taste. You also may have to cut back on, or avoid, many foods you have routinely bought in the past. Keep the following Delgado guidelines in mind in this order of importance:

1. The first rule would be to consume less than 100 mg. of CHOLESTEROL in a day (zero cholesterol intake would be even better). High cholesterol accounts for more deaths in the U.S.than all other causes combined.

2. The second rule is to keep your FAT intake between 10 and 20 grams per day while you're trying to lose weight, and never more than 40 grams a day if you are at your ideal weight. It would be better to avoid any food with 4 or more grams of fat per serving.

3. PROTEIN is the #3 enemy when used in excess. Keep your protein intake between 40 and 80 grams a day. If protein is the first ingredient of any food item, it is probably too concentrated for regular use. Center your diet around complex carbohydrates (starches, fruits and vegetables) and not around protein from meat, chicken, fish, eggs, milk, cheese or nuts.

4. The fourth rule is to cut back on excessive calories from SUGAR. If sugar is listed near the beginning of the ingredient list, or if sugar is listed under different names, then you should rarely use the product. Simple carbohydrates (sugars) should be limited to less than 25 grams a day.

5. The fifth rule is to keep total SODIUM intake per day between 2000 to 4000 mg. Use less than 200 mg. of sodium per serving for low sodium diets and less than 600 mg. for moderate use.

6. The sixth rule is to reduce or avoid CAFFEINE AND ARTIFICIAL ADDITIVES.

Not all additives are harmful, but many have not been thoroughly tested long enough on humans to assess their safety. Buy organic whenever possible, and if the label lists too many ingredients of which you are not sure, then it would be better to avoid that product.

The rules above are listed 1 through 6 in order of importance so that you realize it would be safer to cheat occasionally on a food with slightly more sugar or salt, than to cheat with foods higher in cholesterol and fat.

The final concept to follow when making food selections is to decide whether a food has redeeming value. Foods that are advertised as having "no cholesterol" or "low salt" may not have any positive value. You should ask the following questions to determine the food value: Does this food have fiber in it? (We need 40 to 60 grams of total fiber a day). Is the food unprocessed? Is the food high in complex carbohydrates? (Your body needs at least 200 grams or more of carbohydrates a day to operate efficiently).

Now let me take you through a supermarket, starting with the produce section.

15

SUPER MARKET
FIELD TRIP

PRODUCE SECTION

The best section of the supermarket for weight loss is produce. Try out a variety of vegetables and fruits. Cucumbers (Japanese and English) are very good, high in Vitamin E and natural nutrients. They have 13 calories per 3 ounce serving and are high in Vitamin C, iron and fiber. Go through the bell pepper section - try red, green and yellow bell peppers. Try different types of lettuce - romaine, leaf, butter, etc. There is even an organic section in some supermarkets where you can get organic carrots, lettuce, etc. Look at the different types of cabbages, leeks, collard greens, mustard greens - all highly nutritious green leafy vegetables. Broccoli is tasty raw or cooked. I love to carry cherry tomatoes with me because they are so convenient and easy to eat. There are a variety of mushrooms that are very nutritious. I buy green China peas, also known as snow peas, and eat them raw. They are flavorful and sweet. Asparagus are great. I like to get microwaveable vegetables such as broccoli, potatoes, carrots and snow peas, in their container. You can just pop them into the microwave and cook for a few minutes, then add your own low-fat, favorite toppings or sauces and make them even better. You can get sprouted seeds like sprouted sunflower seeds and bean sprouts that are very nutritious. If you like turnips, rutabagas or eggplant, they're all low in calories and of course low in fat. There are many types of squash - Italian, yellow and summer - and all types of potatoes are very good for weight loss. Try some fresh herbs baby dill, oregano, sage or parsley. Cilantro is an excellent herb and adds much flavor to Mexican dishes.

Cantaloupes, honeydew and watermelon are always good choices, as are fresh pineapple, papaya and pink grapefruit. Grapes - red or green seedless - are low calorie items and bananas are great for a weight loss plan. Try different types of pears, apples and all citrus fruits. Some larger markets carry plantain bananas, kiwis, mangos and the more exotic fruits.

SOUPS
★★ = Good; ★ = OK; X = No Good

NOTE: These products were reviewed July, 1991; however, food producers periodically change ingredients. Therefore, our recommendations may change accordingly.

   X   CAMPBELL'S CHICKEN RICE - Has 6 grams of fat, 160 calories and is 34% fat. It contains chicken meat and chicken fat. It is too high in fat to eat regularly.

   ★   SALT REDUCED CHICKEN NOODLE SOUP - 2 grams of fat and 70 calories. It does have 26% fat. Since it is 2 grams of fat per container (2 servings), you might use this on a limited basis. It also lists the ingredients as enriched egg noodles, which contain some cholesterol. I would use this on a very limited basis, if at all. When you are purchasing soups, make sure to select items that are not the "cream of" variety. If they don't list the grams of fat be very cautious.

★ ★ **PROGRESSO SOUP** - Starts off its ingredient list with beef stock, beef, carrots, potatoes, red kidney beans, great northern beans, lima beans, green peas, celery, cabbage and salt. Near the end they list beef fat and olive oil. It is hard to decide how much oil has been added to the product. It may be acceptable if after you open the can and refrigerate it, you can spoon off the fat that comes to the top. That would reduce the fat significantly and you could use it safely. There are other good soups if you can find them.

★ ★ **BAXTER'S SCOTCH LEEK SOUP** - Has no added fat. Baxter's soup comes from Scotland and certain stores carry it. Contact us if you're having difficulty finding it.

★ ★ **PRITIKIN SOUP** - It has less than 1 gram of fat per 70 calories, making it under 5% fat and it does have under 175 mg. of sodium. You might want to add some extra spices to flavor it up a bit, but it is a very low-fat soup that can be used as often as you like.

You can make your own lentil bean soup and different types of soups using various vegetables. You'll do really well if you eat soups daily.

CANNED FRUITS / VEGETABLES / JUICES

★ ★ **NO SUGAR APPLESAUCE** - Is always a good diet selection with almost no fat, very tasty and refreshing.

★ ★ **CANNED PEACHES** - Buy them with no added sugar in their juice.

★ ★ **CRUSHED PINEAPPLE AND SLICED PEARS** - Good items to add variety to your plan.

★ ★   **JUICES** - You might want to try tomato juice or V-8. The sodium content is a little high, but it's acceptable. These juices are lowfat, and zero in cholesterol. You may be able to find "sodium free" tomato or V-8 juice in the diet section of your market.

READ THE LABELS on canned vegetables. Make sure the tomatoes, peas, corn, etc. don't have much added sugar. Some canned vegetable products are acceptable. They may have added salt; still, by simply pouring off the juice, you are reducing the sodium content to a tolerable level. You can get asparagus that are pickled, just pour off the juice.

GRAINS, RICE AND NOODLES

★ ★   All the different types of whole grain cereals are good. However, check the fat and sugar content. Some traditional granolas have added oil, so read the labels. The puffed cereals and hot oat bran are generally the lowest calorie of all the cereals, so they are great for weight loss if you like to eat them. The whole grain hot cooked cereals are also good for weight loss; just read the labels to find if they have added sugar. Avoid added sugar and the instant quick cereal. You should have whole grain - they're the better products to use.

★ ★   **RICE CAKES** - You can get rice cakes of various types that are good for you.

★ ★   **BROWN RICE** - Fast cooking quick brown rice like Uncle Ben's retains all its nutrients. Try to avoid white rices. Go with California Brown Rice - short grain or long grain. MJB has a quick brown rice that is an acceptable product.

★ ★   **MISC. RICES** - Basmati is a rice from India that is a whole grain rice, though it's white in color. CousCous

Pilaf is a type of wheat product that is very tasty and used in the Middle East. It is zero fat and 100 calories, so you know it's less than 2% fat.

★ ★ **NOODLES** - When you buy noodles, make sure you don't buy just the Durham Wheat. Durham is a type of wheat, it doesn't mean it's a whole grain. It should say "whole wheat" - that is important to look for.

BEANS

There are many good dried beans - lima, kidney and pinto; split peas, lentils and barley. Cook them and add flavor with your favorite spices.

BREAD SECTION

★ **SEVEN GRAIN BREAD** - Is baked fresh daily at my local supermarket. The ingredients are wheat flour, rye flour, whole wheat flour, oat flakes, millet seed, flaxseed, sesame seed, molasses, salt, lactic acid, ascorbic acid and a fungal amylase. This is a good tasting bread and although it's not 100% whole grain, it does have a few whole grain items in it. This would be a good product. It is important that you buy whole grain bread without added milk, eggs, etc.

★ ★ **HOMEMADE BREAD** - I have recently purchased a bread maker (Hitachi brand) that makes marvelous bread in 4 hours. It only takes me five minutes to put in the ingredients (1 1/8 cups water, 2 cups whole grain pastry flour, 1/2 cup oat flour blend, 1/2 cup multi blend flour, 1/2 oz. Butter Buds, 3 tablespoons of applesauce or apple juice concentrate, and 1/4 oz. Fleishmann's Rapid Rise yeast.) The machine mixes, rises and bakes the bread ready to eat.

★ **OAT BRAN MUFFINS** - You should always ask the baker what is in the product if there isn't an ingredient list. I've noticed when I've asked in the past, the oat bran muffins do contain egg yolks. Unless they are labeled as low cholesterol, they'll have cholesterol from the egg yolks in the batter. Muffins with no yolks and no added oil are available if you check labels closely.

★ ★ **LOW CHOLESTEROL OAT BRAN MUFFINS** - Although they have low cholesterol, they might have quite a bit of oil added to them, so be careful about the grams of fat. If you can't get an ingredient list from the baker, then I would choose to avoid them and get another product where there is an ingredient list so you know what's in it.

★ **ROMAN MEAL BREAD** - When you buy bread, be sure to read the ingredient list. Ideally the first ingredient is whole grain. For example, Roman Meal lists its first ingredient as wheat flour bleached, which is not a whole grain. Then it has selected wheat bran and whole wheat flour, molasses and whole rye. It's okay overall - the fat content is less than 1 gram of fat with 70 calories. So bread, in general, is low in fat.

★ ★ **BLACK RYE BREAD** - There is an Orowheat black bread from Europe that is a good whole grain bread. It has a lot of fiber and you might enjoy its extra texture.

X **DOUGHNUTS** - Be careful to avoid bakery goods like doughnuts. It may seem obvious, but a list of ingredients in doughnuts includes enriched flour, soy bean and cottonseed oil, beef fat, lard, egg yolks, cocoa and sodium calcinate. Doughnuts are very high in fat and sugar as you would expect.

FROZEN FOODS

★ ★ **FROZEN GREEN PEAS** - There are some brands available with 0 grams of fat and about 60 calories - that would be less than 5% fat. You can find frozen vegetables without added salt. Be careful to avoid added butter or salt. Green peas are a great source of fiber, complex carbohydrates, vitamins and minerals.

★ ★ **LEAF SPINACH** - Has 0 grams of fat, 25 calories

and is less than 2% fat. It has 140 mg. of sodium per 1/3 cup serving that is low and no salt added.

★ ★ **CHUCKWAGON CORN** - 1 gram of fat per 90 calories. Ingredients are corn, red bell peppers, green bell peppers and onion. Percentage of fat is less than 10%. Somehow, people have been led to believe corn is fattening. However, corn has virtually no fat in it. We would encourage you to use more frozen, canned or fresh vegetables if you're trying to lose weight.

★ ★ **FROZEN BLUEBERRIES** - A great item to select with no sugar added. These are great because you can put them in a container and eat them as they defrost during the day. Even when other fruits are out of season, these blueberries are marvelous, sweet and tasty and you can eat them all day.

★ ★ **PITTED DARK SWEET CHERRIES** - No sugar added and they are in their natural fruit juice. These are really tasty.

★ ★ **FROZEN BOYSENBERRIES** - Have no sugar added and less than a gram of fat per serving.

★ ★ **FROZEN SLICED FREESTONE PEACHES** - No sugar added, excellent on cereal.

★ ★ **FROZEN RED RASPBERRIES AND FROZEN STRAWBERRIES** - Also very good choices.

These fruits make a marvelous variety of good, tasty items to snack on during the day. Frozen fruits are also low in fat, calories and sodium with no cholesterol. Fruits, especially berries, contain a rich supply of fiber and water.

HEALTHY CHOICE - Provides a frozen food line advertised as low fat, low cholesterol, low sodium.

★ **ORIENTAL PEPPER STEAK DINNER** - Lists on the label 6 grams of fat for the entire package. They have already calculated the percentage of total calories on this product and they listed it at 18% fat. My guidelines recommend anything under 20% fat as acceptable, so this meets the guidelines of a low-fat product. This product has 60 mg. of cholesterol. You want to have less than 100 mg. of cholesterol in a day. If you had this TV dinner, you should restrict your intake of any other foods containing cholesterol that day. In this way, you are always taking in less cholesterol than your body gets rid of each day.

This product has 510 mg. of sodium. Actually, anything under 175 mg. of sodium per serving is considered very low. However, they are calling this a "serving per container" - the entire container is an 11 ounce serving. I consider 300 mg. to 500 mg. moderate to low sodium for a food product. So, 510 mg. per the entire serving is moderately low in sodium. We will compare that to some other frozen meal items.

They have broken down the polyunsaturated fat and the saturated fat on the product, but this is not as significant as looking at the total grams of fat. We are more concerned you reduce your total fat intake instead of the type of fat (i.e., polyunsaturated, saturated, etc.).

The ingredients are beef sirloin, beef broth, broccoli, apples, cooked rice, water, green peppers, sugar, water chestnuts, soy sauce, modified food starch, carrots, raisins, tomato paste, flavoring, butter, salt, soy bean oil, spice, corn syrup, milk, cream sauce, whey and caramel color. It does have some ingredients that might set off your alert button to think, "Wait a minute, maybe I don't want this product." Compared to other frozen foods, we'll make some judgments about this item. In deciding whether the Oriental Pepper Steak is good for weight loss, consider that there are other foods with less fat, protein and cholesterol that would be a better choice for regular use. We recommend you use this product on a limited basis, no more than once a week. We can compare this to another Healthy Choice dinner with less fat.

★ HEALTHY CHOICE CHICKEN ORIENTAL DINNER - You will find this frozen dinner is even better from a calorie and weight loss standpoint, because it has only 2 grams of fat and 5% of its calories come from fat. That is considerably less than Pepper Steak, which has 18% fat and 6 grams of fat. The sodium in this is 460 mg. and that is still considered low. The cholesterol content is 55 mg. They are almost identical in cholesterol - the other dinner contained 60 mg of cholesterol.

The ingredients in this dinner are water, chicken breasts, broccoli, pineapple, cooked rice, red and green pepper, zucchini, chicken broth, sugar, soy sauce, modified food starch, carrots, water chestnuts, tomatoes, bamboo shoots, brown sugar, butter, flavoring, salt, spice, soy bean oil, corn syrup, sauce, milk, cream sauce and whey. For anyone who is allergic to milk, even a small amount of added milk would be enough that you may not want this product. However, this dinner has been divided into three different compartments. The milk is in a cream sauce which is easily identified, so you would know to avoid it if you were allergic to milk products. All cream sauces should be avoided to reduce your fat and cholesterol intake.

X WEIGHT WATCHER'S BEEF SALISBURY STEAK ROMANA WITH ROTTINI NOODLES - This item has 13 grams of fat per 8.75 ounce serving. It has 320 calories, with over 36% of its calories coming from fat! This is considerably higher in fat. Cholesterol is slightly high at 80 mg. With Weight Watcher's name brand, you think immediately, "This must be an acceptable product." However, when you read the total grams of fat, and if we keep in mind we are trying to have less than 20 grams of fat in the entire day (keeping it to 2, 3 or 4 grams of fat per serving) this is actually high in fat with 13 grams of fat coming from one meal. The ingredients start with cooked enriched macaroni product (not a whole grain - just enriched), cooked beef, tomato puree, tomatoes, salt, skim mozzarella cheese, zucchini, onion, yellow squash, mushrooms, eggs, green peppers, hydrogenated liquid soy bean oil, breadcrumbs, parmesan cheese, spice, corn oil, Worcestershire sauce, artificial flavors, chicken, meat, sugar, monosodium glutamate (MSG), xanthine gum, dried whey, lemon concentrate and tumeric. If you read the ingredient list, you should consider avoiding this product because it has excessive fat, cholesterol and salt from MSG. MSG can cause an allergic reaction in some people. This product contains many undesirable ingredients and should be avoided.

★ **LEAN CUISINE CHICKEN CHOW MEIN WITH RICE** - It has 5 grams of fat, 250 calories and 1,030 mg. of sodium. It doesn't list the cholesterol content of the product. The ingredients are cooked white rice, water, cooked chicken, bean sprouts, soy sauce, onions, bokchoy, chestnuts, green peppers, mushrooms, red peppers, chicken fat, sugar, soy bean oil, salt, MSG, caramel coloring, chicken broth, tumeric and natural flavors. This product can be used on a limited basis because it has 5 grams of fat for the entire serving and 18% of its total calories from fat. The sodium content is high, and you also will have to decide if you're willing to go with white rice versus brown rice. For an occasional meal, it's acceptable.

X LEAN CUISINE DELUXE FRENCHBREAD PIZZA - It has 12 grams of fat, 340 calories and 1,080 mg. of sodium. With 12 grams of fat, we multiply the 12 X 9 and we divide that by 340 and we come up with 32% fat. Now we're already above what we consider to be a low-fat product. Our guidelines recommend under 20% fat; however, this product is 32% fat. The ingredient list includes beef, pork, Italian sausage, MSG, skim milk, cheese, corn oil, margarine and chicken fat. This list is virtually all fat. Does it have any redeeming nutritional value - does it have any whole grain? It's made with French bread, which is not a whole grain bread, so you would have difficulty finding any redeeming quality. The only ingredient of any nourishing value is the tomato sauce! In summary, we would not choose to eat this product and add 12 grams of fat to our day's intake with no nutritional benefit.

X O'BOY ITALIAN BREAD WITH CHEESE - It has 11 grams of fat (11 X 9 = 99). It has 202 calories (100 divided by 202), which would make it over 50% fat. The sodium content per serving is 494 mg. and there are 4 servings in this container. Therefore, that would be close to 2000 mg. of sodium if you ate all four servings. You should avoid this product. You can invent your own Italian sandwich with whole grain sourdough bread, Liteline or Lifetime cheese microwaved on top, and Enrico's or Johnson's no-fat spaghetti sauce.

X SWANSON'S FRIED CHICKEN AND WHIPPED POTATOES - It has 21 grams of fat and 390 calories. We always tend to think of chicken as something that is good for us and low in fat. But, if we read the label, it's shocking to find out how high in fat fried chicken actually is. If we calculate the percentage of fat, it turns out to be 48% fat.

X SWANSON'S FRIED CHICKEN (DARK PORTION DINNER) - It has 28 grams of fat and that is per 9-3/4 ounce serving at 560 calories. If you multiply 28 X 9 and divide by 560, we find this has a whopping 45% fat and 1100 mg. of sodium per serving. With this frozen dinner you get 2 pieces of chicken, whipped potatoes, corn and a brownie.

X STOUFFER'S DINNER SUPREME GLAZED HAM STEAK IN SAUCE - With 15 grams of fat and 380 calories, we know this is nearly 50% fat. It has 1,960 mg. of sodium. So far this is the highest concentration of sodium we have examined, which would be quite a significant amount of sodium and fat comparatively.

X SWANSON'S MACARONI & CHEESE - Has 21 grams of fat, which now exceeds everything we've compared so far. If we multiply 21 X 9 and then divide by the 400 calorie serving, it has 47% fat. It has oil, milk and cheese, which all contribute cholesterol and fat to this artery-closing product.

X BIRDSEYE FETTUCINI ALFREDO WITH SOUR CREAM AND PARMESAN CHEESE - 14 grams of fat, 220 calories, 460 mg. of sodium per serving and it's calculated at 57% fat. Ingredients are enriched noodles (not a whole grain), egg yolks, parmesan cheese, cheese culture and nonfat dry milk. It's very concentrated in dairy product, fat and cholesterol and they didn't even list the cholesterol content. I'm sure they don't want you to know how much cholesterol it has. Always avoid cream or cheese sauces added to noodles or vegetables.

X SUGAR FREE ESKIMO PIE - This is a vanilla frozen dairy dessert. It has 12 grams of fat with 140 calories. 69% of its calories are in fat. Its ingredients include (in the coating), coconut oil, chocolate and nonfat dry milk. In the vanilla portion it has milkfat, nonfat dry milk, cellulose gum and several other additives. There are 12 grams of fat per bar and if you were to eat all six bars in this package, you would polish off 72 grams of fat!

★ ORANGE/VANILLA TREAT - This is an artificially flavored frozen bar. Ingredients are skim milk, sugar and corn syrup and has 1 gram of fat with 60 calories. The percentage of fat would be 15% and that is considerably lower in fat than some other Weight Watcher products we have compared. If you're allergic to milk, then you may not want to use this item since milk is the first ingredient. If you're not allergic, then using this product in small quantities would be acceptable.

★ FRUIT AND YOGURT BAR - This item has less than 1 gram of fat, and 70 calories. It is under 12% fat. Ingredients are yogurt, strawberries, water, sugar, milk, corn syrup, cream, natural flavors and stabilizers.

★ WELCH'S NO SUGAR ADDED FRUIT JUICE BARS (Grape, strawberry and raspberry) - This has 0 fat with 25 calories. Zero would mean it has less than 0.3 grams of fat. This is a very acceptable item. The ingredients are grapes, water, grape juice and guargum, which is a carbohydrate thickener. It is made with NutraSweet (aspertame) and if you're not using any other products made with NutraSweet, then this product could be used once or twice a week as a dessert.

★ **FROZEN FRUIT-CHUNKY STRAWBERRY** - It has 0 grams of fat, 16 grams of carbohydrate and 70 calories. It's less than 4% fat. Ingredients are strawberries, strawberry puree, water, fructose, sucrose, natural vegetable stabilizer and colored with beet juice. This is a good product. There are no artificial flavorings in it; still, it does have fructose and sucrose that are two types of sugars that can elevate triglycerides. Its total fat content is low and although it has sugar, your body can handle sugar easier than foods with fat and sodium.

★ **DOLE FRUIT AND JUICE BAR** - Has less than 1 gram of fat and 16 calories. Ingredients are pineapple, pineapple juice from concentrate, water, orange and orange juice, sugar, banana puree, corn syrup, natural flavors, locust bean, guargum, citric acid and tumeric extract. You might be able to find a product with no sugar added. Compared to other frozen desserts, this one would be acceptable.

★★ **FROZEN ORANGE JUICE, PINEAPPLE JUICE, AND APPLE JUICE** products are available with 0 grams of fat. Check for the sugar content and buy the frozen juices with no sugar added.

X COOL WHIP - A nondairy whipped dessert that has 1 gram of fat with 12 calories and is 70% fat. The ingredients include water, corn syrup, hydrogenated coconut palm kernel oil, sugar and sodium casenate. A serving is one tablespoon, so if you have 3 tablespoons, you'd eat about 3 grams of fat. The key is to be able to stop yourself at 3 tablespoons. If you can do that - great, then you can use small amounts of this. It is essentially a non- nutrient item. Consider this as a dessert for occasional use.

X COOL WHIP EXTRA CREAMY WHIPPED TOPPING WITH REAL CREAM - It is 56% fat with 1 gram of fat per 16 calories. It has skim milk as an ingredient, so if you're allergic to milk, it could be a problem. It also has cholesterol in it and they do not list how much. It would be better to avoid it for these reasons.

X MRS. RICHARDSON'S WHITE HOT FUDGE TOFU TOPPING - It has 1 gram of fat and 90 calories - less than 10% fat. Ingredients are water, fructose, corn syrup, sugar, nonfat dry milk solids, cocoa, partially hydrogenated coconut oil, starch, algin, salt and xanthine gum. This product is low in fat per two tablespoons. However, it does have sugar, caffeine and a milk-based derivative. You'll find that the chocolate Hershey syrups and the chocolate syrup type products are actually low in fat. A chocolate product becomes much higher in fat when they turn it into a bar, because it takes oil to form the bar. A chocolate bar has over 12 grams of fat. The chocolate syrup is safer to use on a limited basis. You can get carob syrup at the health food store. Although carob syrup is caffeine-free and low in fat, it is sweetened with fructose, so limit its use.

X KLONDIKE LIGHT FROZEN DESSERT - Is listed on the label as 93% fat free, sugar free and sweetened with NutraSweet. We prefer people not use NutraSweet because of the many reported side effects, including headaches, psychiatric disorders and stimulating the appetite that can cause you to gain weight. Don't be misled by the word "light." This ice cream has 10 grams of fat with 140 calories making it 64% fat - extremely high in fat. I find it very hard to accept how they advertise it as "light." Cholesterol is listed at 10 mg. per bar and there are 6 bars in this package. They've listed it as 93% fat free, simply because they include the fluid, the moisture and listed it by volume and not percentage of total calories. It's a trick many food producers use. They know if you see 93% fat free, you'll think this is automatically low in fat and not look past that. However, if the food product is between 97% and 100% fat free by volume, only then will the fat calories be less than 20%.

★ **DOLE STRAWBERRY FRUIT SORBET -** An ice cream type frozen dessert that has less than 1 gram of fat and 100 calories, so you know it's less than 2% fat. Ingredients are strawberry puree, water, sugar, corn syrup, natural flavors, bean gum, pectin, guargum and beet concentrate. Bean gum and pectin are soluble fibers that lower cholesterol. They are acceptable. The corn syrup and sugar are the only two ingredients that would make a person use this only as a dessert and not to be eaten in large quantities. You can buy sorbet with no sugar added from many health food stores. Sorbet is low in fat and lactose free and has no cholesterol. It's a much better choice over regular ice cream.

X TOFUTTI - 7 grams of fat per 150 calories and it has 42% of its calories in fat. Its ingredients read: pure cane sugar, tofu, strawberries, corn syrup and corn oil. We would consider this a high-fat item. Tofutti is advertised as cholesterol free; however, because of the fat and high sugar, we would not use this on a regular basis as a dessert.

X MOCHA MIX ICE CREAM - A nondairy frozen dessert with 7 grams of fat per 140 calories. It is advertised as containing no cholesterol, 100% milk free and no lactose, however, it is high in fat at over 45%. Ingredients are water, sugar, corn syrup and soy bean oil. The first three ingredients (besides water) are sugars and oil, then the strawberries. I would not consider this a diet food.

X HAAGEN DAZ VANILLA ICE CREAM - Has 17 grams of fat, 260 calories and 55 mg. of sodium. The sodium is low; however the percentage of fat is 59%. It's no surprise the label does not list the cholesterol content. Ingredients are fresh cream, skim milk, cane sugar, egg yolk and natural vanilla flavor. They put both cream and egg yolk in Haagen Daz and each yolk adds over 213 mg. of cholesterol. This is an ice cream you should never buy.

X SWANSON'S FRENCH TOAST WITH SAUSAGE - It has 21 grams of fat and 380 calories, making it 50 % fat and 560 mg. of sodium. Ingredients: (French toast) milk, eggs, cream, sugar, butter, natural flavor and sausage. The cholesterol content is not listed; however, based on the ingredients we can estimate this product is dangerously concentrated in artery-clogging cholesterol.

★ NUTRIGRAIN EGGO WAFFLES WITH WHOLE GRAIN - 5 grams of fat per 130 calories. It has 35% of calories in fat, so if you use this at all it would be on a limited basis, no more than once a week. Enriched wheat flour is the first ingredient, then hydrogenated soy bean oil, egg white and whole wheat. It's advertised as whole grain, but the whole wheat isn't listed until fourth. Its main ingredient, enriched wheat flour, is not a "whole" grain.

X CHEESE SWEET ROLLS - Weight Watcher's Microwave Breakfast has 24% fat, 5 grams of fat per 190 calories and 20 mg. of cholesterol. This is a product you should avoid as well.

DELI/CHEESE SECTION

X JIMMY DEAN'S PORK SAUSAGE - Has 13 grams of fat, 140 calories per cooked patty and is 83% fat. By percentage, sausage is one of the highest fat products we've reviewed so far. Ingredients: pork, ham, loins, water, salt, spice, sugar and MSG. It doesn't list the cholesterol content for obvious reasons. The cholesterol content is very similar to other meats (approximately 20 mg. of cholesterol per one link).

★ BREAST OF TURKEY - Is advertised as 95% fat free. It does have 1 gram of fat, 35 calories and is 20% fat by total calories. Turkey breast meat is the first ingredient, then salt, sugar and garlic powder. Turkey breast is low in fat, the cholesterol content is listed as 20 mg. per 1 ounce serving. It is for this reason that turkey should be used only on a limited basis as flavoring for other dishes and not as the main dish. Turkey also lacks fiber and complex carbohydrates.

X CREAM CHEESE - It advertises 1/2 the calories of butter and margarine. It has 10 grams of fat and 100 calories that makes it 90% fat and it also has 90 mg. of sodium per one ounce serving. Its ingredients are cream cheese, salt and guargum. They're bragging it's half the calories of butter - wait until we compare butter! We would not buy this product.

X LITE PHILADELPHIA CREAM CHEESE - It lists 25% less fat than regular cream cheese. It has 7 grams of fat, 80 calories that makes it by percentage 78% fat and it does have 25 mg. of cholesterol per 1 ounce serving. They're bragging here about a product that is high in fat!

X LAND O'LAKES SHREDDED CHEDDAR CHEESE - 9 grams of fat per 110 calories for a 1 ounce serving and 74% fat. You'll find most all cheeses (Jack, Cheddar, Swiss) are between 60 and 80% fat, contain 30 mg. of cholesterol per ounce (1 1/2 slices) and up to 400 mg. of sodium. It is unfortunate people use cheese as a main ingredient in so many dishes. If you must use cheese, try LiteLine or Lifetime cheese. Better yet, don't use this high cholesterol, high fat product at all. People who eat cheese are at a much greater risk of developing cancer, arthritis, diabetes, high blood pressure, stroke, heart disease and several other degenerative diseases.

X TURKEY FRANKS - You may think because they're made with turkey, that they'll be low in fat. However, the percentage is 76% fat, 11 grams of fat, 130 calories and 630 mg. of sodium per link. It does not list the cholesterol content. This is a very high fat item, though they advertise it as 80% fat free. Remember, that is by volume, so it's not as low in fat as you're led to believe. Don't buy them.

X   OSCAR MAYER BOLOGNA - The chief ingredient is pork with 13 grams of fat, 140 calories, 30 mg. of cholesterol and 480 mg. of sodium. It's 84% fat and one of the highest fat items we've compared.

★   SLICED TURKEY - Has 3 grams of fat per 50 calories. Remember, the rule of thumb is to keep your fat intake to 3 grams or less per serving. Although sliced turkey is high by percentage of fat (54%), you could ocassionally use it in a smaller portion serving, since it has only 3 grams of fat.

X   BOB'S BIG BOY BLEU CHEESE SALAD DRESSING - It's famous! It has 6.8 grams of fat with 66 calories making it 93% fat! Its number one ingredient is mayonnaise, followed by sour cream, bleu cheese, buttermilk, soy bean oil, vinegar, salt, spices, xanthine gum and MSG. We would not recommend you use this fatty dressing.

X   BOB'S ROQUEFORT SALAD DRESSING - Has 6.4 grams of fat and 63 calories. 91% fat with mayonnaise, sour cream, roquefort cheese, soy bean oil and MSG making a dangerous combination.

X   BOB'S TARTAR SAUCE AND DIP - Is over 9 grams of fat and 86 calories and 96% fat. Use this sauce and you'll get fatter because mayonnaise is the number one ingredient.

★   LITELINE AMERICAN FLAVORED CHEESE - Has 2 grams of fat and 50 calories. Its percentage of fat is 36% and has 10 mg. of cholesterol. It's above the 20% fat content we would generally allow; however, the grams of fat are less compared to other cheeses. It's at least 1/3 the amount of fat and much lower in cholesterol. You might use this on a limited basis in small quantities.

X   PARMESAN CHEESE - Per ounce, has 7 grams of fat and 120 calories. Its sodium content is 450 mg. per ounce. It has 53% fat, so if you did use parmesan cheese, you would only sprinkle a little onto your food, remembering it is high in fat.

X VELVETTA PROCESSED CHEESE SPREAD - A food product that is very high in fat. With 6 grams of fat, it calculates out at 68% fat per 1 ounce serving. Keep that in perspective - an ounce is a very small portion. This container has 32 ounces of cheese, and most people will eat more than an ounce per meal. A typical recipe may call for four ounces of cheese and that works out to 24 grams of fat, an excessive amount.

★ DANISH HAM WITH NATURAL JUICE - Has less than 1 gram of fat. This one is advertised as 98% fat free and it has 45 calories. This comes out to 20% fat by total calories, instead of the 2% by volume they list on the label. However, this would be acceptable in small quantities.

POULTRY SECTION

X ZACKY FARMS CHICKEN - Is advertised as 100% natural California grown. Skin included, it has 22 grams of fat, 450 calories and 44% fat. Though it is chicken, it's high in fat. Also, chicken has nearly as much cholesterol as red meat.

X FRESH GROUND TURKEY - Is advertised as 93% fat free. However, it has 6 grams of fat, 120 calories - making it 45% fat.

X PHYLLIS GEORGE'S CHICKEN BY GEORGE (tomato herb with basil) - It has vegetable oil listed as an ingredient in the sauce. With 7 grams of fat and 190 calories, this is an item that is 33% fat. I don't want people to get the impression that just because it's chicken or turkey you should eat it in unlimited quantities. They do have a high fat content. You should use chicken only as a flavor or a condiment added to grain, vegetable casseroles, etc. and not as the main dish.

★ TURKEY SELECT FRESH BONELESS TURKEY BREASTS - "99% fat free" with 1 gram of fat, 90 calories, which works out to actually 10% fat. This is a lower fat item than the other cuts that we've compared. When it is lean meat and lower in fat, it still has just as much cholesterol permeated throughout the white part of the meat. You can use it, but in small quantities.

DAIRY SECTION

X I CAN'T BELIEVE IT'S NOT BUTTER - Although it has no cholesterol as advertised, it has 10 grams of fat per 90 calories and that is in one tablespoon making it 100% fat. All margarines are virtually all fat and would be very harmful to anyone who is trying to maintain good circulation and lose weight. The sodium content is 90 mg. per tablespoon.

X SHEDD'S SPREAD - Is a vegetable oil base margarine with no cholesterol. It has 7 grams of fat with 70 calories making it over 90% fat. With no carbohydrate and no protein, it has 99% of its calories coming from fat.

X FLEISCHMAN'S LIGHT CORN OIL SPREAD - Is made from 100% corn oil. It is over 99% of its calories from fat with 8 grams of fat per tablespoon and 80 calories. It has 70 mg. of sodium. The fact they've listed it as "light" is very misleading. Don't buy the product just because it has the word "light." It is a very concentrated fat, as high in fat as all other butters and margarines we've compared.

X WEIGHT WATCHER'S REDUCED CALORIE MARGARINE - It has 6 grams of fat and 50 calories. Using our fat equation of 6 grams X 9 divided by 50 calories, it is 108% fat. (Rounded out to 100%.) This proves how misleading the Weight Watcher's "Reduced Calorie" concept is in this case. It advertises 50% less fat and calories, and that it's sweet and unsalted. The ingredient list is liquid soy bean oil, partially hydrogenated soy bean oil, mono and diglicerides (which is another name for fat), potassium sorbet, citric acid and artificial flavors. This is a very high fat product; don't buy it if you're trying to lose weight.

X HEART BEAT - Claims to be 75% less fat. It has 3 grams of fat and 25 calories, which makes it 100% fat. There is zero protein and zero carbohydrates. Water is added to dilute the fat volume. The public is being mislead by products such as this. Don't buy it - it's all fat and it may worsen your heart and your health.

X KNUDSEN'S SOUR CREAM - 13 grams of fat and 130 calories. It's over 90% fat.

X KNUDSEN'S NICE 'N LIGHT SOUR CREAM - 6 grams of fat, 90 calories with over 60% of its calories coming from fat. This is nearly as bad as regular sour cream. Be sure to avoid this product.

X IMO SOUR CREAM SUBSTITUTE - Has 3 grams of fat, 30 calories per tablespoon and 90% fat. If you could hold yourself down to a tablespoon, you might get by. However, with the impression it's low in fat, you may overuse this product, so I would not buy it.

X JELLO PUDDING CHOCOLATE/VANILLA SWIRL - Has 6 grams of fat, 170 calories with no cholesterol and 125 mg. of sodium. It is 32% fat, so limit its use.

X TAPIOCA PUDDING - Has 7 grams of fat and 170 calories, which tells you that it's 35% fat. It is moderately low in sodium at 140 mg.

★ LOW FAT COTTAGE CHEESE - It lists 2% milkfat, 2 grams of fat in 100 calories, making it 18% fat. Since it's below the 20% category that we've listed, you could use this in moderation. But, keep in mind that if you are allergic to milk cottage cheese could cause a problem for people with its ingredient list of skim milk, milk, cream and salt.

★ ALTADENA NONFAT PLAIN YOGURT - It's listed as less than 1 gram of fat and 100 calories, which makes it less than 2% fat. If you're not allergic to milk, then this nonfat yogurt would be acceptable to be used in small quantities in dips and on potatoes.

★ **WEIGHT WATCHER'S YOGURT** - Lists 0 grams of fat and 90 calories making it less than 2% fat. It would be best not to use this concentrated milk product no more than once a week.

X **KNUDSEN'S OR YOPLAIT YOGURT** - Has about 4 grams of fat and 240 calories that works out to 15% fat. However, they are both high in sugar content. When they add sugar, it changes the percentage because sugar adds appreciable calories and when you divide the number of fat grams into the total calories, it makes it appear lower in fat than it truly is. For example, in Knudsen's Lowfat Yogurt, sugar is the third ingredient listed, after milk and skim milk. You then have to look at the grams of fat. When you see 4 grams of fat per 8 ounce serving, you're above what I consider to be a reasonable intake. Some other yogurt products have 0 to 3 grams of fat, so you could use them in small quantities. Keep in mind that if you're allergic to milk, yogurt will cause you similar gastrointestinal problems. Although yogurt is easier to handle for most people than milk, it can cause some severe allergic reactions.

X **MOCHA MIX** - Has 2 grams of fat, 20 calories per tablespoon and calculates out to 90% fat. Water is the first ingredient followed by soy bean oil and corn syrup. Most people use this product in their coffee, and generally use more than just a tablespoon. I've seen people adding too much of it to cereal, fruit and desserts. This would add a lot of fat to their diet. This item should be avoided or restricted in use though it has no cholesterol.

X **JERSEYMAID HALF AND HALF** - Has 2 grams of fat, 20 calories per tablespoon and it's 90% fat, the same as Mocha Mix. You get the same fat in Mocha Mix as you do in Half and Half!

X **LOW-FAT MILK** - Has 5 grams of fat and calculates out to 32%. Though it lists just 2% by volume on its label, that makes it deceptively attractive when it's actually high in fat.

★ **VITAMITE** - A nondairy product with 5 grams of fat and 110 calories is 41% fat. For those people who are allergic to milk and dairy products, Vitamite may be an acceptable product to use in small quantities. But, try not to drink it in excess because it is high in fat.

X GOAT'S MILK - Has 8 grams of fat and 150 calories, making it 48% fat. You have to remember that milk from an animal like a goat or cow has to have a considerable amount of fat because it was intended to allow for the rapid growth of a large animal. A goat or a cow grows to full size in a year. They grow much faster than a human being who takes nearly 20 years to reach full size. Avoid goat's milk unless you are a goat!

★ **LACTATE NONFAT MILK** - Titled as lactose reduced, it has under 1% fat. It has zero grams of fat and 90 calories. A word of caution for people who are allergic to milk - even though the lactose has been reduced, you may still be allergic to the over 28 different milk proteins. The high protein content of milk also could worsen osteoporosis or kidney damage. Limit lactate nonfat milk to less than 2 glasses a day.

★ **JERSEYMAID NONFAT MILK** - It is listed as nonfat, with 1 gram of fat and 90 calories, but it calculates to 10% fat.

X JERSEYMAID EGGNOG - Ingredients include Grade A whole fat milk, cream, sugar, nonfat milk, corn sweeteners, egg yolks, natural and artificial flavoring. We would prefer you not use eggnog during the holidays if you want to keep your cholesterol and fat intake down. They don't even list the grams of fat on this product which would be considerable. Keep in mind that egg yolks are high in cholesterol and fat.

X EGGS - An egg yolk has 213 mg.!* of cholesterol and over 70% fat. Eggs have been publicized as an ideal source of protein; however, the Egg Board promotes studies using rats to prove their claims. Recent studies using humans show that eggs are not the high quality protein we once believed. Avoid egg yolks at all times. Try Scramblers or Egg Beaters as a safe alternative.

  * The U.S.D.A. has recently lowered its estimate of eggs cholesterol content from 274 mg. to 213 mg.

DRESSINGS / OILS

  X MIRACLE WHIP LIGHT MAYONNAISE CHOLESTEROL FREE - It has 80% fat and 4 grams of fat per tablespoon for 45 calories. This is a very high fat item that you must limit or avoid.

  X BEST FOODS CHOLESTEROL FREE REDUCED CALORIE MAYONNAISE - Is 90% fat. It has 5 grams of fat per 50 calories. Limit your use to less than 1/2 tablespoon a day.

  X EXTRA LIGHT VIRGIN OLIVE OIL - Has a fat content of 14 grams, 130 calories per tablespoon and 100 % of its calories are in fat. It is unfortunate how they get away with labeling it "extra light" (referring to light in color) when its fat content is identical with other oils.

  X VEGETABLE OILS - If we look at corn oil, safflower oil, Mazola, Crisco, etc., they are all 100% fat. You would be smart to avoid all oils if you are trying to keep your weight and fat intake down. They also will cause your triglycerides to elevate and cause you to gain weight quickly.

MISCELLANEOUS

  ★ ★ SUNDANCE DRINKS - These are good drinks because they are pure juice made with no added fructose or sugar. They contain white grape juice, kiwi, lime and sparkling water.

  X NEW YORK SELTZER - Ingredients are carbonated water, high fructose corn syrup and natural flavors. Beware of fructose sweeteners because they tend to elevate triglycerides more than any regular sugar and they contribute calories to your intake. Try to buy the mineral waters that are flavored without the fructose - just the juice and water.

X   RUFFLES POTATO CHIPS - 10 grams of fat per 150 calories making it 60% fat. It does have 190 mg. of sodium per ounce and the package is 7 ounces. It's a high fat, high sodium product. Potatoes are the main ingredient, with various types of vegetable oils added.

★ ★   GREAT AMERICAN PRETZEL - 1 gram of fat and 110 calories making it under 8% fat. Pretzels are traditionally low in fat because they are baked. The sodium content is 150 mg. per ounce. You can find pretzels with light salt or no sodium added. (Less than 175 mg. of sodium per serving is desirable.

X   CALIFORNIA POPCORN - Is advertised as the alternative to junk food. It has 6 grams of fat, 140 calories and it is low sodium at 100 mg. It is 39% fat. The reason the fat content is high is because they have added corn oil with cheddar cheese to the popcorn. You can get hot air popcorn with no added fat and that would be a much better choice.

X   MICROWAVE POPCORN WITH REAL BUTTER (frozen) - There are 8 grams of fat with 140 calories. It has 135 mg. of sodium that is low per 3-cup serving. However, it has 51% of its calories in fat. Popcorn is the primary ingredient, along with vegetable oil, cottonseed or soy bean oil, butter and salt. This is why hot air popcorn, or a lower fat microwave popcorn would be a better choice.

X   ORVILLE REDENBACHER'S NATURAL MICROWAVE POPCORN (frozen) - Has 8 grams of fat, 140 calories and 310 mg. of sodium per 3 serving bag. Our guideline of 0-3 grams of fat per serving has been exceeded with 8 grams of fat. When we then calculate the percentage of fat, it is 51%, so you should not buy any product like this.

X   NEWMAN'S POPCORN - Has 8 grams of fat, 150 calories and that would make it a high fat item at 48%.

★ ★   WEIGHT WATCHER'S MICROWAVE POPCORN - Has 1 gram of fat and 80 calories, making it under 11% fat. This would be a good choice.

X   WEIGHT WATCHER'S ROASTED PEANUTS - 7 grams of fat with 100 calories, which calculates to over 63% fat. Again, you have to read the labels, even if it's a Weight Watcher's brand name, it could be high in fat.

X   FIGURINES - A diet bar that has 5 grams of fat with 100 calories, making it 45% fat. The fat added is supposed to suppress your appetite. We would not use these "diet bars."

★ ★   BUTTER BUDS - A good item to add in place of regular butter. It has maltodextrin (carbohydrate), salt, spray dried butter flavor, guar gum (fiber), and baking soda. One packet (1/2 oz.) has 48 calories, less than one gram of fat, no cholesterol and 680 mg. of sodium. Use less than one packet in a day to control your sodium intake.

★ ★   MRS. DASH'S SPICES - These are very good. I like the table blend and extra spicy flavors.

★ ★   PRITIKIN SALAD DRESSING - These are better for you than most other brands. Still, you need to try other low-fat brands to match your taste preference.

★   KRAFT NO-OIL ITALIAN DRESSING - A good dressing with no added fat. It has a little bit of sodium and some additives, but it is tasty, and you can use it on a limited basis.

X   RICHARD SIMMONS SALAD SPRAY ITALIAN - 1 gram of fat and 14 calories. Ingredients are water, white wine vinegar, soy bean oil, sugar and apple juice concentrate. It is 64% fat. Because it's a spray, you can get by with using a lot less, however, it is high in fat. Avoid it!

Richard Simmons, how could you put your name on such a high fat product?

★ ★ **CHILI SALSAS** - Have no added fat and you can even find some with low sodium. Even those with some salt added are within acceptable limits.

★ ★ **MUSTARDS** - Add much flavor to your diet. Mustard seed does have approximately 50% fat; but, mustard has less than one gram of fat per tablespoon and it is so strong and flavorful that you get by with using a lot less in your average recipes. We encourage you to use mustard if you do like it.

★ ★ **JELLIES** - You might want to buy some different jellies and spreads. Simply Fruit by Smucker's is a good one because it uses white grape juice, blueberries, lemon juice concentrate and fruit pectin. It has no added fat, sugar, artificial color or flavoring. It makes a good item to add taste and variety. You can get raspberry, blueberry and other flavors.

★ **MANISCHEWITZ POTATO PANCAKES** - Adds a good flavor. Pour them in a bowl, mix with water and microwave. The label doesn't list the fat content, but we have written to them and found that potato pancakes are acceptable (if they're not fried in oil), less than 15% fat. This product is slightly high in sodium.

★ ★ **CORN TORTILLAS** - Are very low in fat and high in fiber.

X FLOUR TORTILLAS - Are higher in fat (3-7 grams) than corn tortillas and inadequate in fiber.

★ **WHOLE WHEAT FLOUR TORTILLAS** - Have 4 grams of fat, 140 calories and 26% fat. You may find whole wheat tortillas made with less oil, and under 3 grams of fat per serving.

X CHICKEN CHILI W/BEANS BY STAGG - Has a fat content of 7 grams and 300 calories and that makes it 32% fat.

X   PHYLLIS DILLER'S CHICKEN CHILI - Doesn't list the grams of fat on the label. It has chicken, soaked beans, water, tomatoes, tomato paste, salt and chili peppers. There is no added oil and it is hard to figure out how much fat is in the chicken itself, but it looks to be a little bit lower in fat than some other chili beans.

X   SPAGHETTI O'S WITH SLICED FRANKS AND TOMATO SAUCE - Has a fat content of 9 grams and 220 calories, making it over 37% fat.

SPAGHETTI SAUCE

★ ★   ENRICO'S ALL NATURAL - Has 1 gram of fat per 60 calories, making it an excellent choice at 15% fat.

X   PREGO - Has 32% fat with 5 grams of fat per serving. Avoid the entire line of Prego sauces.

★   HOMESTYLE RAGU - Has an acceptable 2 grams of fat. However, most of the Ragu line of sauces are high in fat.

Try to look for spaghetti sauces with 0, 1 or 2 grams of fat. READ THE LABELS!!!

GROCERY LIST

(HEALTH FOOD STORE USUALLY STOCKS) "H"

REPLACE DAIRY PRODUCTS WITH:

H   Amazake Rice Milk
H   Soy Milk
H   Almond Milk

GRAINS, BEANS AND PEAS

Quaker Old-fashioned oats
Mother's oat bran cereal
Nutri-Grain cereal

Wolff's Kasha - roasted buckwheat kernels
Natural Ry-Krisp crackers
Wasa Brod crisp rye bread
Whole Earth 100% whole wheat snack twists
Bohemian Hearth Stoneground 100% whole wheat bread
Lady Lee lentils
Lady Lee popcorn (other brands are fine if no fat is added)
Lady Lee green split peas
California brown rice
Valley Farms lentils
Pita whole wheat bread by International Baking Co.
Corn tortillas
Good Stuff grainola bread
Evans long grain brown rice
Mr.Pita pocketbread
Albertson's eight whole grain breads (other multigrain breads are fine)
Nabisco spoon-size Shredded Wheat
Kings crisp bread
H DeBoles Wheat-free corn pasta
H Stone-Buhr 7 grain cereal
H Olde Mill brown rice flour
H Arrowhead Mills steel-cut oats
H Food for Life Ezekiel bread
H Hale N' Hardy whole wheat spaghetti
H Lifestream Essene raisin bread

H   Lifestream Essene fruit cake
H   Back to Nature sprouted 7-grain banana crisp whole grain cereal

READY-TO-EAT FOODS

Manischewitz potato pancake mix
Orowheat seasoned dressing
Manischewitz unsalted matzo meal
Carroll Shelby's Original Texas Chili

H   Hummus
H   Tabouli
H   Johnson's spaghetti sauce
H   Tumaro's sweet and sour vegetables
H   Tumaro's Chinese rice
H   Tumaro's 2 bean tamales and enchiladas
H   Bible burger
H   Legume tofu manicotti
H   Legume tofu lasagna
H   Legume tofu pizza

CANNED AND FROZEN VEGGIES

Whole kernel corn
Birds-Eye stir fry vegetables
Rosarita vegetarian refried beans
Del Monte burrito filling mix
Westpac frozen oriental vegetables
Anderson split pea soup
Health Valley split pea soup
El Pato tomato sauce
Kroger whole kernel golden corn
Campbell's crispy Spanish soup

Dennison's chili beans
Ortega green chili salsa
Pritikin tomato soup
Pritikin ribbon pasta
Rosarita enchilada sauce
Frazier Farms sweet peas
Pritikin chicken soup
Chun King sliced water chestnuts
Coop garbanzos
Progresso Roman beans
Progresso crushed tomatoes

SPICES

Pure and Simple picante salsa
Herbs and spices without salt
McIlhenny Co. Tabasco sauce

FRUITS

Big Valley freestone peaches
Dole chunk pineapple
Diet Delight cling peaches
Country Life apple butter
Minute Maid 100% pure lemon juice

LIMITED OR OCCASIONAL USE
Weight Watcher's ice cream
A-1 steak sauce

16

COMPOSITION OF FOODS CHART

NOTE: Foods with less than .1 mg. or .1 gm. in any category (fat, protein, etc.) are listed as 0. If the information is not available, the notation will be -. Additional information on vitamins and minerals is available through the U.S. Government Composition of Foods; however, we have provided the information that is most pertinent to your goals of weight loss and cholesterol reduction.

We have listed the foods in order of lowest fat, calories, and cholesterol in the beginning on up to the highest, most harmful foods at the end. Abbreviations for food categories are CAL (calories), CHO (carbohydrates), PRO (protein), NA (sodium), TF (total fiber), SF (soluble fiber), CHOL (cholesterol). All measurements are in grams, except cholesterol and sodium which are measured in milligrams.

VEGETABLES
1 cup serving, raw
(unless otherwise noted)

	FAT	CAL	CHO	PRO	NA	TF	SF	CHOL
Watercress,1 sprig	0	0	0	.1	1	1	.4	0
Parsley,10 sprigs	0	3	.7	.2	4	2	.7	0
Romaine lettuce,4 lvs	0	8	.8	.8	4	.6	.2	0
Iceberg lettuce,4 lvs	0	12	2	.8	8	.6	.2	0
Onions	0	48	11	2	0	5	3	0
Beets,cooked	0	52	12	2	84	4	1	0

	F A T	C A L	C H O	P R O	N A	T F	S F	C H O L
Water chestnuts,8	.1	38	9	.5	10	.4	-	0
Radish,10	.2	7	2	.3	11	1	.2	0
Endive	.2	8	2	.6	12	1	.5	0
Alfalfa sprouts	.2	10	1	1	2	4	-	0
Cucumber	.2	14	3	.6	2	1	.4	0
Cabbage	.2	16	4	.8	12	1	.8	0
Celery	.2	16	2	.6	70	3	.8	0
Green peppers	.2	18	4	.6	4	2	.5	0
Cauliflower	.2	24	5	2	14	3	2	0
Eggplant,cooked	.2	26	6	.8	12	4	2	0
Zucchini	.2	28	7	1	4	4	2	0
Pumpkin,cooked	.2	48	12	2	4	4	1	0
Okra,cooked	.2	50	12	3	8	5	2	0
Carrots	.2	50	11	2	50	5	2	0
Artichoke,1	.2	53	12	3	79	15	2	0
Swiss chard	.3	26	2	3	125	1	-	0
Red peppers	.3	31	7	1	4	2	.8	0
Tomato	.3	33	7	2	4	.8	.2	0
Dill pickle,1	.4	11	2	.7	1428	.7	.3	0
Turnips,cooked	.4	28	8	1	88	3	2	0
Turnip greens	.4	30	6	2	42	2	.7	0
Leeks,cooked	.4	32	8	.4	5	3	1	0
Kale	.4	34	6	2	30	4	2	0
Collards	.4	36	7	3	2	2	1	0
Bamboo shoots	.4	36	7	4	6	1	-	0
Spinach,cooked	.4	42	6	6	126	4	.9	0
Green snap beans	.4	44	10	2	4	3	.8	0

	F A T	C A L	C H O	P R O	N A	T F	S F	C H O L
Sauerkraut	.4	44	10	2	1560	5	2	0
Rutabaga,cooked	.4	58	13	2	30	3	2	0
Summer squash	.6	36	8	2	2	1	.5	0
Asparagus	.6	44	8	5	8	5	1	0
Brussel sprouts	.6	66	12	7	36	8	3	0
Winter squash	.8	78	18	2	2	7	.7	0
Mushrooms,10	.1	50	8	4	10	4	.5	0
Broccoli	.2	24	4	2	24	5	2	0
Potato,cooked	.2	134	31	2	8	3	2	0
Yams	.2	158	36	2	12	8	4	0
Green peas	.6	122	21	9	3	3	-	0
Parsnips,cooked	.8	126	30	2	16	6	.8	0
Corn,cooked	2	180	42	6	28	8	3	0

BEANS/PEAS
1 cup serving, cooked

Lentils	0	212	39	16	26	4	2	0
Split peas	.3	230	42	16	26	10	3	0
Pinto beans	.6	204	37	13	13	11	4	0
Lima beans	.6	208	40	12	28	9	2	0
Kidney beans	.8	206	36	14	6	12	5	0
Navy beans	1	224	40	15	13	3	-	0
Black-eyed peas	1	198	30	14	8	25	11	0
Garbanzo beans	4	396	49	16	35	3	-	0
Soybeans	12	254	20	22	26	3	-	0

FRUITS
1 cup serving
(unless otherwise noted)

	F A T	C A L	C H O	P R O	N A	T F	S F	C H O L
Loquat,1	.1	5	1	.1	.1	1	-	0
Kumquat,1	.1	12	3	.2	1	1	-	0
Grapes,10	.1	15	4	.2	.1	.4	.1	0
Peach,1	.1	37	10	.7	.1	5	1	0
Passion fruit,1	.2	18	4	.4	5	2	-	0
Lime,1	.2	20	7	.5	1	.3	-	0
Fig,1	.2	37	10	.4	1	.6	-	0
Tangerine,1	.2	37	9	.6	1	2	.5	0
Grapefruit,1/2	.2	38	10	.8	.1	2	.6	0
Casaba melon,1/10	.2	43	10	2	20	1	-	0
Honeydew melon,1/10	.2	46	12	.6	13	1	-	0
Cranberries	.2	46	12	.4	1	4	1	0
Orange,1	.2	62	15	1	.1	1	.3	0
Crabapple,1	.3	83	22	.4	1	.7	-	0
Lemon,1	.4	22	11	1	3	6	1	0
Rhubarb	.4	26	6	1	4	4	1	0
Kiwi fruit,1	.4	46	11	.8	4	1	-	0
Boysenberries,frzn	.4	66	16	1	2	5	-	0
Plum,1	.5	36	9	.6	.1	.6	.2	0
Guava,1	.5	45	11	.8	2	5	-	0
Apricot,3	.5	51	12	1	1	2	1	0
Apple,1	.5	81	21	.3	1	3	1	0
Starawberries	.6	45	10	1	2	1	-	0
Blackberries	.6	74	18	1	.2	9	1	0

	F A T	C A L	C H O	P R O	N A	T F	S F	C H O L
Blueberries	.6	82	20	1	9	5	.6	0
Cherries,10	.7	49	11	.9	.1	1	.3	0
Watermelon	.7	50	12	1	3	-	-	0
Raspberries	.7	61	14	1	.1	-	-	0
Nectarine,1	.7	67	16	1	.1	2	.5	0
Pineapple	.7	77	19	.6	1	2	.6	0
Pear,1	.7	98	25	.7	1	5	1	0
Cantaloupe,1/2	.8	94	22	2	23	1	-	0
Gooseberries	.9	67	15	1	1	7	1	0
Applesauce,unswtd	.2	106	28	.4	5	4	1	0
Dates,10	.2	228	61	2	2	2	-	0
Persimmon,Japanese	.4	118	31	1	3	3	-	0
Plantain,cooked	.4	178	48	1	8	-	-	0
Pomegranate,1	.5	104	27	2	5	.3	-	0
Papaya,1	.5	117	30	2	8	4	1	0
Prunes,10	.5	201	53	2	3	12	4	0
Banana,1	.6	105	27	1	1	2	.6	0
Mango,1	.6	135	35	1	4	2	.5	0
Elderberries	.8	105	27	1	.2	10	-	0
Raisins	.7	434	115	5	17	16	4	0
Olives,green-6	5	45	1	.6	936	1	-	0
Olives,black-6	12	121	2	1	550	1	-	0
Avocado	30	306	12	4	21	-	-	0

CEREALS
1 ounce serving, cold

Puffed Rice,1C	.1	57	13	.9	0	.2	.1	0

	F A T	C A L	C H O	P R O	N A	T F	S F	C H O L
Grape Nuts,1/4C	.1	101	23	3	197	2	.5	0
Kellogg' Corn Flakes,1C	.1	110	24	2	351	.4	.1	0
Corn Chex,1C	.1	111	25	2	271	.4	.2	0
Special K,1 1/2C	.1	111	21	6	265	.8	.2	0
Rice Chex,1 1/8C	.1	112	25	2	237	.1	-	0
Product 19,3/4C	.2	108	24	3	325	1	.3	0
Golden Grahams,3/4C	.2	109	24	2	364	.2	-	0
Rice Crispies,1C	.2	112	25	2	340	.1	-	0
Shredded Wheat,1 lg biscuit	.3	83	19	3	0	3	.4	0
Grape Nuts Flakes,7/8C	.3	102	23	3	218	2	.5	0
Nutri-Grain,wheat	.3	102	24	3	193	2	.3	0
Trix,1C	.4	109	25	2	27	.1	-	0
All Bran,1/3 C	.5	71	21	4	320	9	2	0
Wheaties,1C	.5	99	23	3	354	3	.5	0
Life,2/3C	.5	104	20	5	148	1	.3	0
Total,1C	.6	100	22	3	352	3	.5	0
Wheat Chex,2/3C	.7	104	23	3	190	3	.5	0
Honey Nut Cheerios,3/4 C	.7	107	23	3	257	-	-	0
Kix, 1 1/2 C	.7	110	23	3	339	.2	-	0
Kellogg's RaisinBran,3/4C	.7	115	28	4	269	1	-	0
Bran Chex,2/3C	.8	91	23	3	263	6	1	0
Corn Bran,2/3C	1	98	24	2	244	6	2	0
Cheerios,1 1/4C	2	111	20	4	307	2	.7	0
C.W.Post,1/4C	4	126	20	3	49	-	-	0
Nature Valley Granola,1/3C	5	126	19	3	58	-	-	0
Quaker 100% Natural,1/4C	6	133	18	3	12	-	-	0

HOT CEREAL
1 cup cooked,w/o salt

	F A T	C A L	C H O	P R O	N A	T F	S F	C H O L
Cream of Rice	.1	126	28	2	2	-	-	0
Farina	.2	116	25	3	1	-	-	0
Malt-o-Meal,plain or chocolate	.3	122	26	4	2	-	-	0
Cream of Wheat,reg.	.5	134	28	4	2	-	-	0
Cream of Wheat instant	.6	153	32	4	6	-	-	0
Wheatena	1	135	29	5	5	-	-	0
Oats,reg.,quick, or instant	2	145	25	6	1	4	2	0
Maypo	2	170	32	6	9	-	-	0

BREADS,
without eggs or dairy products
1 serving

	F A T	C A L	C H O	P R O	N A	T F	S F	C H O L
Rye bread,1 slice	.3	63	13	2	144	.9	.3	0
Pumpernickel,1 slc	.3	64	14	2	148	4	.6	0
Corn tortilla,1	.5	32	6	.8	3	-	-	-
Whole wheat bagel	.6	152	32	5	360	-	-	0
Whole wheat bread, 1 slc	.8	63	12	3	137	1	3	0
White bread,1 slc	.8	70	70	2	132	.5	.2	0
Soda cracker4,	1	35	6	.7	88	-	-	-
Saltine cracker,	1	52	9	1	132	-	-	0
Whole wheat English muffin,1	2	130	26	5	171	-	-	0

	F A T	C A L	C H O	P R O	N A	T F	S F	C H O L
Whole wheat pancake	3	74	9	3	0	-	-	0
Graham cracker,2	3	107	20	2	188	3	.5	0
Bran muffin,1	5	126	20	5	178	-	-	0
Buckwheat pancake,1	5	135	18	5	338	-	-	0
Waffles,2	5	204	32	6	599	-	-	0
Plain pancake,1	6	62	22	5	417	-	-	0

GRAINS
1 cup serving, no salt added (unless otherwise noted)

White rice,2/3C ckd	.1	149	33	3	10	.2	.2	0
Wild rice,2/3C ckd	.2	78	17	3	11	-	-	0
Popcorn	.4	31	6	2	.2	-	-	0
Macaroni,ckd	.6	154	32	5	1	1	.3	0
Spaghetti,ckd	.6	155	32	5	1	2	.5	0
Brown rice,2/3C ckd	.8	156	33	33	16	3	.3	0
Whole wheat pasta,ckd	1	174	37	7	2	-	-	0
Egg noodles,ckd	2	200	37	7	1	-	-	50
Bulgur,dry	2	628	139	15	7	-	-	0
Pot/Scotch barley,dry	2	696	154	19	8	-	-	0

BRAN
1 ounce, (6 tbsp.)

Psyllium (Metamucil)	-	180	-	-	1	20	16	0
Corn Bran	-	-	-	-	-	6	2	0
Wheat bran	2	40	16	4	0	14	2	0
Oat bran	2	110	16	6	0	4	2	0
Wheat germ	3	108	14	8	1	-	-	0
Rice bran	5	100	9	4	tr	10	3	0

NUTS/SEEDS
4 ounce serving

	F A T	C A L	C H O	P R O	N A	T F	S F	C H O L
Chestnuts,roasted	2	280	60	4	4	-	-	0
Pumpkin seeds	48	592	15	38	652	-	-	0
Sunflower seeds	56	648	21	26	4	-	-	0
Peanuts,rstd,sltd	56	660	21	30	492	9	.1	0
Almonds,rstd,sltd	58	888	28	9	668	14	2	0
Pistachios,rstd,sltd	60	688	31	17	888	-	-	0
Cashews,rstd,sltd	64	652	37	18	728	-	-	0
Walnuts	64	688	14	28	0	5	1	0
Pecans,rstd,sltd	74	748	25	9	888	7	1	0
Brazilnuts	75	744	14	16	0	9	1	0
Filberts,rstd,sltd	75	752	20	11	888	8	1	0
Macadamias	84	796	16	10	4	-	-	0

SOUPS
10 ounces, canned

	F A T	C A L	C H O	P R O	N A	T F	S F	C H O L
Beef broth,bouillon	.5	16	.1	3	782	-	-	0
Chicken broth	1	39	.9	5	776	-	-	0
French Onion,Knorr	1	56	-	-	1156	-	-	0
Minestrone, Maneschewitz	1	83	-	-	108	-	-	0
Pritikin soups	1	130	-	-	200	-	-	0
Vegetable,Health Valley	1	133	-	-	613	-	-	0
Campbell's Home Cookin'	1	150	-	-	1050	-	-	0

	F A T	C A L	C H O	P R O	N A	T F	S F	C H O L
Gazpacho	2	57	.8	8	1183	-	-	0
Chicken w/rice, Campbell's	3	80	8	5	1030	.1	.1	9
Chicken noodle, Campbell's	3	88	10	5	1138	.1	.1	9
Vegetarian vegetable, Campbell's	3	100	15	4	975	.1	.1	0
Tomato,Campbell's	3	113	20	4	838	-	-	0
Minestrone,Progresso	3	168	28	7	767	.3	.2	0
Clam Chowder,Snow's	4	160	22	11	875	0	0	8
Lentil,Progresso	4	179	24	11	819	4	2	4
Cream of Mushroom, Lipton	5	118	14	4	1263	0	0	2
Black Bean, Health Valley	5	213	33	9	573	4	1	0
Split Pea w/ham Campbell's	5	222	32	12	997	5	2	4
Ham w/bean, Campbell's	9	260	-	-	1097	-	-	-

BEVERAGES
1 cup serving
(unless otherwise noted)

Club soda	0	0	0	0	75	0	0	0
Diet soda	0	0	.4	0	76	0	0	0
Ginger ale	0	113	29	0	25	0	0	0
Seven-up	0	144	36	0	4	0	0	0
Cranberry juice	0	147	37	0	5	0	0	0
Cola drink	0	151	38	0	15	0	0	0

	F A T	C A L	C H O	P R O	N A	T F	S F	C H O L
Tea	0	0	0	0	29	0	0	0
Coffee,6 ounces	0	3	.5	0	2	0	0	0
Grape juice	0	89	22	.1	0	0	0	0
Apple juice	0	92	23	.7	12	0	0	0
Orange juice	0	92	23	.8	58	0	0	0

LIQUOR

Red/white wine, 3 1/2 ounces	0	70	1	0	7	0	0	0
Gin,whiskey,rum, vodka,1 ounce	0	97	0	0	.4	0	0	0
Beer, 12 ounces	0	151	13	1	25	0	0	0
Cordials,liquers, 1 ounce	.1	74	8	0	1	0	0	0

POULTRY
3 1/2 ounces serving, roasted (organ meats are stewed) (unless otherwise noted)

Goose liver,1	4	125	6	15	132	0	0	-
Pheasant	4	133	0	24	37	0	0	-
Chicken gizzard,1	4	153	1	27	67	0	0	194
Quail	5	134	0	22	51	0	0	-
Duck liver,1	5	136	4	19	-	0	0	-
Chicken,white meat w/o skin	5	173	0	31	77	0	0	85
Chicken drumstick,1	6	112	0	14	47	0	0	48
Chicken liver,1	6	157	1	24	51	0	0	631
Turkey liver,1	6	169	3	24	64	0	0	626
Chicken wing,1	7	99	0	9	28	0	0	29

	F A T	C A L	C H O	P R O	N A	T F	S F	C H O L
Chicken heart,1	8	185	.1	27	48	0	0	242
Turkey,white meat	8	197	0	29	63	0	0	76
Chicken,dark meat w/o skin	10	205	0	27	93	0	0	93
Chicken,white meat	11	222	0	29	75	0	0	84
Turkey,dark meat	12	221	0	28	76	0	0	89
Chicken,dark meat	16	253	0	26	87	0	0	91
Goose	22	305	0	25	70	0	0	91

SEAFOOD
3 ounce serving; baked, broiled or steamed (unless otherwise noted)

	F A T	C A L	C H O	P R O	N A	T F	S F	C H O L
Shrimp	.9	102	2	20	133	0	0	167
Surgeon caviar, teaspoon	2	26	.7	5	352	0	0	55
Crab,hard shell	2	89	.5	16	422	0	0	95
Scallops	3	85	3	13	425	0	0	29
Cod	3	100	.3	17	331	0	0	50
Flounder	3	101	.3	17	340	0	0	50
Haddock	3	102	.4	18	322	0	0	59
Snails	3	111	2	18	31	0	0	57
Abalone	3	120	4	19	15	0	0	55
Perch	4	110	.3	18	341	0	0	55
Pike	4	110	.3	18	313	0	0	55
Bass	4	117	.4	20	376	0	0	56

	F A T	C A L	C H O	P R O	N A	T F	S F	C H O L
Clams	5	93	2	10	326	0	0	40
Lobster	5	111	.2	15	398	0	0	78
Frog legs,2	6	121	9	8	239	0	0	78
Oysters	6	134	10	9	372	0	0	46
Tuna	6	155	.3	25	299	0	0	56
Swordfish	7	148	.4	20	369	0	0	56
Catfish	7	149	.5	19	491	0	0	59
Salmon	7	149	.4	21	380	0	0	36
Carp	9	161	.5	19	472	0	0	59
Sardines,cnd in oil	9	172	0	20	700	0	0	102
Halibut	9	214	0	31	168	0	0	75
Trout	14	217	.3	21	342	0	0	55
Mackerel	15	213	.3	19	336	0	0	94
Herring	15	222	.4	19	377	0	0	95
Eel	22	286	5	15	88	0	0	51

SALAD DRESSINGS/SAUCES
2 ounce serving

	F A T	C A L	C H O	P R O	N A	T F	S F	C H O L
Vinegar	0	8	4	0	0	0	0	0
Good Seasons No Oil Italian Mix	0	12	-	-	60	0	0	0
Weight Watcher's French	0	15	-	-	345	0	0	36
Pritikin No Oil	0	24	-	-	20	0	0	0
Soy sauce	0	44	6	6	4416	0	0	0
Horseradish	0	24	6	.8	56	0	0	-
Catsup	.4	64	15	1	624	0	0	0
Kraft Catalina Reduced Calorie	1	32	-	-	240	0	0	0

	F A T	C A L	C H O	P R O	N A	T F	S F	C H O L
Barbeque sauce	1	47	8	1	5	0	0	0
Wish Bone Lite Russian	1	50	-	-	280	0	0	0
Wish Bone Lite French	4	60	-	-	140	0	0	36
Mustard	4	60	4	4	780	0	0	0
Oriental Chef Tangy Soy	8	70	-	-	480	0	0	0
Wish Bone Lite Ranch	8	90	-	-	300	0	0	16
Kraft 1000 Island	10	110	-	-	305	0	0	16
Kraft Catalina French	12	140	-	-	360	0	0	36
Seven Seas Viva Italian	14	140	-	-	640	0	0	0
Hidden Valley Ranch	16	160	-	-	280	0	0	16
Newman's Own	18	160	-	-	160	0	0	0
Homemade Vinegar/Oil 2 parts oil, 1 part vinegar	19	166	-	-	0	0	0	0
Mayonnaise	44	396	2	.8	314	0	0	32

DESSERTS

	F A T	C A L	C H O	P R O	N A	T F	S F	C H O L
Honey Hill Nonfat Frozen yogurt,3/4 C	0	120	-	-	0	0	0	6
Angel food cake, 1pc. (1/12)	.1	146	33	3	73	2	1	0
Fig bars,1	.9	57	12	.6	40	4	1	8
Dole fruit sorbet, peach,4 ounces	1	110	27	1	10	2	1	0
Tofutti Lite,3/4 C	1	135	-	-	-	-	-	0
Chocolate chip cookie	2	47	7	.5	40	-	-	1
Sugar cookie,1	2	71	12	.8	41	-	-	4
Oatmeal cookie,1	3	54	6	.8	30	-	-	5
Shortbread cookie,1	3	75	10	1	9	-	-	12

	F A T	C A L	C H O	P R O	N A	T F	S F	C H O L
Chocolate cake,1pc.	4	131	23	2	146	-	-	29
Sponge cake,1pc.	4	193	36	5	113	-	-	172
Brownie,1	5	50	21	2	50	-	-	13
Boston cream pie,1pc.	6	207	34	4	175	-	-	64
Banana cake,1pc.	7	247	43	3	180	-	-	38
Rice Dream,3/4 C	8	205	-	-	-	-	-	-
Ice Bean.3/4 C	14	235	-	-	-	-	-	-
Pound cake,1pc.	14	351	49	6	271	-	-	149
Fruitcake,1pc.	15	433	71	6	170	-	-	37
Apple pie,1pc.	22	457	67	4	355	-	-	0
Haagen Dazs,3/4 C	24	395	-	-	-	0	0	-
Cheesecake,1pc.	25	406	37	5	531	-	-	92
Carrot cake,1pc.	28	478	53	5	170	-	-	92

"LEAN AND FREE BEEF"
3 1/2 oz.

New York Strip,1	1	100	0	23	-	0	0	35
Sirloin	1	100	0	22	-	0	0	50

MEATS
3 ounce serving; broiled,lean cuts
(unless otherwise noted)

Sweetbreads	3	143	0	28	99	0	0	396
Vienna sausage,1	4	45	.4	2	152	0	0	8
Pork sausage,1 link	4	48	.1	3	168	0	0	11
Canadian bacon,2 slcs	4	86	2	11	719	0	0	27
Leg of lamb	4	117	0	18	44	0	0	56

	F A T	C A L	C H O	P R O	N A	T F	S F	C H O L
Beef liver,braised	4	137	3	21	60	0	0	331
Veal cutlet	4	140	.7	26	247	0	0	106
Lamb chop,loin	5	116	0	17	186	0	0	58
Ham,lean	5	133	.1	21	1128	0	0	47
Venison	5	153	0	25	338	0	0	70
Veal liver	5	158	5	22	83	0	0	340
Round steak	7	165	0	24	54	0	0	70
Beef bologna,1 slice	8	89	.6	3	284	0	0	16
Pork loin chop	8	166	0	23	56	0	0	71
Tenderloin steak	8	176	0	24	54	0	0	72
Rabbit	8	182	0	25	231	0	0	90
Bacon,3 slices	9	109	.2	6	303	0	0	16
T-bone steak	9	182	0	15	56	0	0	68
Porterhouse steak	9	185	0	24	56	0	0	68
Beef frankfurter,1	13	145	1	5	76	0	0	22
Flank steak	13	207	0	22	70	0	0	60
Lean ground beef	15	238	0	24	76	0	0	68
Shortribs	15	251	0	26	50	0	0	79
Ground beef	17	248	0	23	79	0	0	86
Knockwurst,1 link	19	209	1	8	687	0	0	39
Liverwurst	24	279	2	12	732	0	0	135
Chuck roast	24	301	0	23	50	0	0	84
Kielbasa	31	264	2	12	915	0	0	57

DAIRY AND EGGS
4 ounce serving
(1/2 cup)

Egg white,1 large	0	16	.4	3	50	0	0	0

	F A T	C A L	C H O	P R O	N A	T F	S F	C H O L
Skim milk	.6	90	12	8	126	0	0	6
Buttermilk	2	100	12	8	258	0	0	8
Low-fat fruit yogurt	2	226	42	10	122	0	0	10
Plain low-fat yogurt	2	144	16	4	160	0	0	20
Sherbet	4	270	58	2	88	0	0	14
Egg yolk,1 large	6	63	.04	3	8	0	0	213
Whole egg,1 large	6	79	.6	6	69	0	0	213
2% low-fat milk	6	120	12	8	122	0	0	36
Ice milk	6	184	30	6	106	0	0	18
Plain yogurt	8	140	10	8	104	0	0	28
Whole milk	8	156	10	8	120	0	0	36
Chocolate milk	8	208	26	8	150	0	0	30
Goat milk	10	168	10	8	122	0	0	28
Human milk	10	172	10	8	122	0	0	28
Ice cream	14	268	32	4	116	0	0	58
Evaporated milk	20	338	24	18	266	0	0	74
Eggnog	20	342	38	10	138	0	0	150
Sweetened,condensed milk	26	982	166	24	390	0	0	104
Half and half	28	316	10	8	98	0	0	90
Sour cream	28	492	10	8	124	0	0	102

CHEESES
4 ounce serving

	F A T	C A L	C H O	P R O	N A	T F	S F	C H O L
Low-fat creamed cottage cheese	2	102	4	15	459	0	0	9
Part-skim ricotta	10	170	6	14	154	0	0	38
Mozzarella,part skim	18	328	3	28	528	0	0	64

	F A T	C A L	C H O	P R O	N A	T F	S F	C H O L
Feta cheese	24	300	5	16	1264	0	0	100
American cheese spread	24	328	9	16	1524	0	0	60
Swiss cheese	24	332	2	24	852	0	0	80
Edam	24	404	3	28	1092	0	0	100
Camembert	28	340	.4	22	954	0	0	81
Processed swiss	28	380	2	28	1552	0	0	96
Gouda	28	404	2	28	928	0	0	128
Parmesan	28	444	4	40	1816	0	0	76
Provolone	30	400	2	28	992	0	0	80
Brie	31	380	.4	24	713	0	0	112
Romano	31	440	4	36	1360	0	0	116
Colby	32	380	2	24	684	0	0	92
Bleu cheese	32	400	3	24	1583	0	0	84
Muenster	32	416	1	28	712	0	0	108
Monterey jack	34	424	.8	28	608	0	0	101
Roquefort	36	420	2	24	2054	0	0	104
American cheese processed	36	420	1	24	1624	0	0	108
Cheddar	38	456	2	28	704	0	0	119
Cream cheese	40	396	2	8	332	0	0	124

FATS AND OILS
1/2 cup

	F A T	C A L	C H O	P R O	N A	T F	S F	C H O L
Margarine	91	813	.6	1	1224	0	0	.1
Butter	92	810	0	1	993	0	0	247
Chicken fat	102	920	0	0	0	0	0	88
Veg. shortening	102	920	0	0	0	0	0	0

	F A T	C A L	C H O	P R O	N A	T F	S F	C H O L
Olive oil	109	952	0	0	0	0	0	0
Peanut oil	109	952	0	.1	0	0		
Corn oil	109	960	0	0	.1	0	0	0
Safflower oil	109	960	0	0	.1	0	0	0
Soybean oil	109	960	0	0	0	0	0	0
Sunflower oil	109	960	0	0	.1	0	0	0
Wheat germ oil	109	960	0	0	0	0	0	0

FAST FOODS
1 serving

	F A T	C A L	C H O	P R O	N A	T F	S F	C H O L
McDonald's vanilla								
shake	8	352	60	9	201	0	0	-
chocolate shake	9	383	66	10	300	0	0	9
hotcakes w/butter								
and syrup	10	500	94	8	1070	-	-	59
french fries	11	220	26	3	109	-	-	9
Filet-of-Fish	26	435	36	15	799	-	-	45
Big Mac	35	570	39	25	979	-	-	83
Wendy's chicken								
sandwich	10	320	31	25	500	-	-	59
breakfast sandwich	19	370	33	117	770	-	-	200
baked potato								
w/broccoli/cheese	25	500	54	13	430	5	2	22
Taco Bell taco	9	162	9	12	-	-	-	-
bean/cheese burrito	11	350	48	15	-	-	-	-
Cheese pizza, 1/2 of								
12"pie	12	653	96	39	1347	-	-	-
Arby's roast beef								
sandwich	15	350	32	22	880	-	-	45
Jack in the Box								
Fajita Pita	8	292	29	24	703	1	3	34
Super Taco	17	288	21	12	765	-	-	37

	F A T	C A L	C H O	P R O	N A	T F	S F	C H O L
Egg Rolls (5)	32	675	70	26	1505	-	-	50
Jumbo Jack								
w/cheese	40	677	46	32	1665	-	-	110
Ultimate Cheeseburger	69	942	33	47	1176	-	-	127
Kentucky Fried								
Chicken, 2 pc.combo	35	643	46	35	1441	-	-	180
Burger King onion rings	16	270	29	3	450	-	-	-
Whopper w/cheese	45	740	52	32	1435	-	-	-

17

SAVE YOUR LIFE REDUCE YOUR CHOLESTEROL LEVEL

Your cholesterol level will not affect your weight or your energy level; however, it is a problem that has been tragically overlooked for many years. Cholesterol and atherosclerosis are major problems in America and the overall degree of this problem is not fully understood by our society. We know the death rate from heart disease has decreased slightly; but, it still affects millions of Americans.

Consider the fact strokes are the second leading cause of death. Then combine heart attacks and the number of people who die of strokes and we have diseases that kill more than 50% of all Americans. The pain and the suffering these diseases cause our country is tragic and yet, we continue to ignore dietary treatment. As Americans, it is important that we have the information available to us about the low-fat, zero cholesterol Delgado Plan.

Several years ago I worked with stroke victims in physical therapy in the critical care units. These people had lives just like you and I. They had families. They led happy and successful lives. Then, one unexpected day they had a stroke. Overnight their whole world crumbled and they became bedridden and in need of constant care.

Stroke rehabilitation is a laborious, slow process. It may take six months before a stroke victim can actually walk on their own, and even then many victims never regain full function. Half their body is paralyzed simply because arteries leading to the brain became severely clogged with cholesterol. Consequently, part of the brain dies due to lack of oxygen. Some stroke victims can no longer speak clearly, if that part of the brain was affected. Think about it - the brain never stops working. When you go to sleep, your brain is still functioning and coordinating your whole body.

These are very serious problems: cholesterol, heart disease and strokes. There is a tendency for Americans to ignore something they cannot see. I have conducted over 3,000 seminars in the last 12 years and I spent most of the seminar time educating people about the importance of cholesterol control. When a patient comes to the clinic overweight, fatigued and lacking energy, they immediately know what they want. They want to lose weight and increase their energy. Since we have a solution for them, these people are easy to work with because they will follow the guidelines for losing weight and increasing energy. However, the people with high cholesterol levels don't believe it's a problem.

Cholesterol is the silent killer. Since there are no nerve endings in the arteries, you don't know cholesterol is building up. Unfortunately a massive heart attack or stroke is the first symptom some people will experience. Then you'll seek treatment, but at that point, there is already irreversible damage.

Special interest groups such as the meat, egg and dairy industries are trying to divert attention from their high cholesterol foods by placing the blame on saturated fats. These groups claim palm oil and coconut oil, which are high in saturated fat, are the cause of elevated cholesterol levels. People are now buying vegetable oils high in monounsaturated and polyunsaturated fats mistakenly believing these are better for them.

In the Journal of American Medical Association, March 23, 1990, Vol. 263, Dr. David Blankenhorn of U.S.C. reported his studies on the effects of fats and the development of atherosclerosic lesions in human coronary arteries. The results shocked the margarine and oil industry since it was proven all fats including polyunsaturated, monounsaturated, saturated and fatty acids (lauric, oleic and linoleic acids) more than 26% of calories from fat caused cholesterol lesions in the heart arteries in less than two years. Those people who were protected from cholesterol lesions ate the least amount of all types of fats.

The public is also misled by believing if they avoid saturated fats they can continue to eat their high cholesterol foods. I can't tell you how many people who come to the clinic still eat at least one or two eggs a week, and think it's safe for them. Of course, we know eggs are one of the most potent sources of cholesterol. You should never eat more than one or two eggs per year. That would be only if you were unaware they were in a recipe, such as a bakery item.

I believe part of the reason people continue to eat high cholesterol foods comes from watching television and the brain-washing that conditions them. A study showed that the average person during their lifetime spends:

2 weeks	Speaking with their child (30 seconds per day)
3 weeks	Brushing their teeth
1/3 year	Conversing with spouse (4 minutes per day)
1/2 year	Sitting at red lights
3/4 year	Opening junk mail
1 year	Searching for things they lost
2 years	Exercising (if they exercise one-half hour a day)
3 years	Attending meetings
4 years	Cleaning their house
5 years	Waiting in lines
6 years	Eating
7 years	In the bathroom

23 years   Watching television
            (ASTONISHING!)

The dairy and meat industries promote their products and bombard us with advertising. The average child will watch over 100,000 commercials by the time they're a teenager. These commercials claim eggs, meat and cheese build strong bodies and "milk has something for every body." Commercials about beer, Pepsi, Coke and candy will complete the childs' nutritional education. Spokespersons paid by these special interest groups mislead the public into believing they can eat as much meat, eggs, and cheese as they wish. Deliberately eating these products ignores the fact cholesterol kills more people in America than any other cause of death.

Dr. Wong and Dr. Gold reported the results of their study on over 1,000 youngsters age 2 to 20 (November 1990 American Heart Association Meeting). They found over 53% of children with a dangerously high cholesterol level (200 mg. or higher) watch television two or more hours per day. Those who watched four or more hours per day were four times as likely to have high cholesterol levels.

Cholesterol building up in the arteries is a leading cause of senility. By the age of 60, many senior citizens in our country are completely senile and end up in nursing homes needing constant care. If we look at the issues, we know that cholesterol is the culprit. Even a two-year-old who is fed high cholesterol foods can develop a build-up. By the time he is three, he'll already have fatty streaks in his arteries. That is how early it starts.

In Finland they have the highest cholesterol level in the world and the highest death rate from heart attack and stroke. Their infants are born with a higher cholesterol level than the world-wide averages because the mothers are eating a very high cholesterol diet. In this country our teenagers eat a high cholesterol diet of cheeseburgers, fried foods, beef burritos with added cheese. With all this cholesterol, it's inevitable that a teenager will develop clogged arteries. When they reach 30 or 40 years old, the first heart attacks appear. Every day 3,425 people across the country have a heart attack (1,250,000 per year), and over half these people will die immediately. Heart attacks occur in teenagers, but we don't hear much about them because they're not as frequent as in a 40-year-old. So, we have to start this nutritional plan of zero cholesterol and low-fat intake.

In the last ten years there has been a significant decrease in the number of deaths from atherosclerosis (cholesterol plaques in the arteries). One study estimated that over 180,000 people are alive today in the U.S. because they learned how to lower their cholesterol level, and keep it down. Stop Smoking campaigns have also helped to decrease the death rate. However, the number one causes of death in the U.S. are still heart disease, stroke and cancer.

DEATHS IN 1987

(Most recent year for complete statistics)

Heart Disease, Stroke	908,000
Cancer	476,700
Accidents	92,500
Obstructing lung disease	78,000
Pneumonia & Flu	68,600
Diabetes	37,800
Suicide	29,600
Cirrhosis of Liver	26,000
Atherosclerosis	23,100
AIDS	4,400

At Delgado Medical we are often asked "What is the difference between fat and cholesterol? Fat provides calories; yet, in excess it is the major contributor to obesity and to many diseases that affects our culture. A high fat diet of oils, margarine, whole milk, cheese, meat, etc. can increase the levels of fat in your blood (triglycerides) which leads to the risk of:

1. **HIGH BLOOD PRESSURE** (blood thickened by fat)
2. **ARTHRITIS** (low oxygen from fat causing destruction of joints)
3. **DIABETES** (fat desensitizing insulin causing poor glucose control)

4. **BREAST AND COLON CANCER** (fat causing excessive production of cancer causing hormones and chemicals)
5. **CHRONIC FATIGUE** (high fat levels in the blood that reduces the oxygen carrying capacity of red blood cells to the brain)
6. **GLAUCOMA** (fat increases cortisone levels in the eyes causing swelling, restriction of fluid flow that can result in damage to the retinal nerves of the eye and blindness)
7. **MULTIPLE SCLEROSIS** (fat damages the nerves of the body from reduced oxygen carrying capacity of the blood)
8. **ATHEROSCLEROSIS** (low oxygen levels caused by fat forces more cholesterol deposits into the arteries)

In comparison, cholesterol is much different from fat. First because cholesterol cannot cause you to gain weight since it lacks calories. Unlike fat, you can't see cholesterol in food, since it's permeated equally throughout all animal tissue. This is why there is just as much cholesterol in the white part of chicken or fish as there is in the skin or fat portions. High cholesterol levels can lead to:

1. **ATHEROSCLEROSIS** or narrowing of arteries and capillaries.
2. **HEART ATTACK** from cholesterol blocked arteries to the heart.
3. **STROKE** (clogged and weakened arteries to the brain)

4. **SENILITY** (loss of brain function due to clogged arteries).
5. **IMPOTENCY** (loss of male sexual function due to cholesterol clogging arteries to the penis).
6. **PROSTATE CANCER** (cholesterol build up in the prostate gland restricts oxygen to the gland inducing mutated cancerous cells).
7. **CATARACTS** (lens of the eye fills with cholesterol causing blindness.
8. **GANGRENE** (restricted blood flow to the extremities: fingers, toes, hands and feet, leading to numbness, tissue death and amputation caused by cholesterol build up).
9. **KIDNEY FAILURE** (clogged arteries to the kidneys).

In my book, *Fatigue to Vitality,* and in my audio cassette and video tape series, you can learn more about how to prevent and even reverse diseases such as diabetes, cancer, arthritis, kidney and heart disease. Please contact my office if you don't already have these materials by writing to:

MAILING ADDRESS
DELGADO MEDICAL
16787 Beach Blvd. #202
Huntington Beach, CA 92647
Or call: (714) 540-7725

CLINIC ADDRESS
DELGADO MEDICAL
17150 Newhope St. #217
Fountain Valley, CA 92708

BIBLIOGRAPHY

1. Anderson, James W., M.D. *Diabetes - A practical new guide to healthy living.* New York, New York: Arco Publishing, Inc., 1981.
2. Bailey, Covert. *The Fit-or-Fat Target Diet.* Boston, Massachusetts: Houghton Mifflin Company, 1984.
3. Bennett, Cleaves M., M.D. *In 12 weeks you can control your high blood pressure without drugs.* Garden City, New York: Doubleday & Company, Inc., 1984.
4. Bronfen, Nan. *Nutrition for a Better Life.* Santa Barbara, California: Capra Press, 1980.
5. Burkitt, Denis, M.D., F.R.C.S., F.R.S. *Eat right - to stay healthy and enjoy life more.* New York, New York: Arco Publishing, 1979.
6. Dunne, Lavon J. *Nutrition Almanac.* New York, New York: McGraw Hill Publishing Company, 1990.
7. Guyton, Arthur C., M.D. *Textbook of Medical Physiology.* Philadelphia, Pennsylvania: W.B. Sanders Company, 1976.
8. Klaper, Michael, M.D. *Pregnancy, Children and the Vegan Diet.* Umatilla, Florida: Gentle World Inc., 1987.
9. Langley, Gill, M.A., Ph.D. *Vegan Nutrition.* Oxford, England: The Vegan Society Ltd., 1988.
10. Leonard, Jon N., and J.L. Hofer and Nathan Pritikin. *Live Longer Now.*
11. McDougall, John A., M.D. *McDougall's Medicine.* Piscataway, New Jersey: New Century Publishers, Inc., 1985.
12. McDougall, John A., M.D., and Mary A. McDougall. *The McDougall Plan.* Piscataway, New Jersey: New Century Publishers, Inc., 1983.
13. Pritikin, Nathan. *The Pritikin Permanent Weight Loss Manual.* New York, New York: Grosset and Dunlap, 1981.
14. Pritikin, Nathan. *The Pritikin Program for Diet and Exercise.* New York, New York: Grosset and Dunlap, 1979.
15. Robbins, John. *Diet for a New America.* Walpole, New Hampshire: Stillpoint Publishing, 1987.
16. Sattilaro, Anthony J., M.D. *Recalled for Life.* New York, New York: Avon Books, 1982.

BIBLIOGRAPHY

17. Swank, Roy Haver, M.D., and Barbara Brewer Dugan. *The Multiple Sclerosis Diet Book.* New York, New York: Doubleday, 1977.
18. Webb, Densie, Ph.D., R.D. *The Complete "Lite" Foods Calorie, Fat, Cholesterol and Sodium Counter.* New York, New York: Bantam Books, 1990.
19. Whitaker, Julian M., M.D. *Reversing Diabetes.* New York, New York: Warner Books, Inc., 1987.
20. Whitaker, Julian M., M.D. *Reversing Heart Disease.* New York, New York: Warner Books, Inc., 1985.

ABOUT THE AUTHOR

More than 14 years ago, Nick Delgado was 50 lbs. overweight, had high blood pressure and considered clinically obese. In his search for a solution to his own health problems, he discovered the best approach was a unique nutrition and exercise program. Nick lost 50 lbs. of unwanted fat and reduced his blood pressure and cholesterol to safe levels permanently.

Nick was awarded a full State and University scholastic scholarship to the University of Southern California, where he received a B.A. in Psychology in 1977. He completed six months of Master's work in Physical Therapy at USC's Rancho Los Amigos Hospital in 1977. He went to Loma Linda University in 1982, where he was accepted into their Health Science program as a Masters and Doctoral candidate. Nick worked with the Nathan Pritikin Longevity Center, Santa Monica, California presenting education conferences and scientific studies from 1979-1981. Since then, Nick has professionally conducted 3,200 seminars, workshops and conventions form 1979-1991. Topics have included stress and weight reduction, nutrition, exercise, prevention of disease, quality health and happiness. Nick's goal is to establish health education programs nationally and inter-nationally and in the process help everyone become as healthy and happy as they can.

HERE IS WHAT HEALTH PROFESSIONALS AND PARTICIPANTS SAY ABOUT THE DELGADO PLAN!

Dr. Michael Klaper, M.D.: "In Weight Loss and Energy Now", Nick Delgado presents sound and practical advice for implementing healthful eating into a busy daily life. The wonderful ethnic and other cuisines from which these foods are prepared provide a constant parade of taste delights, that are easy to make and satisfying to enjoy. I recommend it most highly!"

Dr. Joseph Broderick, M.D.: "This book represents the "state-of-the-art" in dietary management of health preservation and disease avoidance (and reversal). Mr. Delgado has taken the principles of diet and exercise fostered by his predecessors and adapted them into a daily living program that is easy, practical and toothsome! I heartily recommend this book to anyone who is truly serious about preserving health and longevity!"

Chuck Satow: "I was running up to 20 miles a week, working out a lot, I was also eating what I thought was a fairly good diet. Just past the age of 40, I was told I had a serious heart condition and that the only solution was a 5-way bypass. After talking with you, I started the program and my cholesterol decreased from 250 down to 172 and has been steadily coming down. Instead of surgery, I went to Mexico on a sailing trip! I find that the people at Delgado Medical are very dedicated."

Louise Washbon: "After coming out of a diabetic coma on 8-11-88 with an impaired memory, I was introduced to your program. I have lost 21 lbs., 2 dress sizes, have my memory, my blood sugar and thyroid all back to normal, I am 54 years young and feel better than I have in years. It's great to be alive!! Thank you!"

Colleen Grajeda: "I lost 42 lbs. in four months and have maintained by weight for 8 years. This is the only program that works for me because it is a way of eating that is good for life."